zest

zest

the very best citrus recipes

The ultimate guide to cooking with oranges, lemons and limes,
including 75 fabulous step-by-step recipes

CORALIE DORMAN

southwater

This edition is published by Southwater

Southwater is an imprint of Anness Publishing Ltd
Hermes House, 88–89 Blackfriars Road, London SE1 8HA
tel. 020 7401 2077; fax 020 7633 9499
www.southwaterbooks.com; info@anness.com

© Anness Publishing Ltd 2004

UK agent: The Manning Partnership Ltd, 6 The Old Dairy, Melcombe Road, Bath BA2 3LR
tel. 01225 478444; fax 01225 478440; sales@manning-partnership.co.uk

UK distributor: Grantham Book Services Ltd, Isaac Newton Way, Alma Park Industrial Estate, Grantham, Lincs NG31 9SD
tel. 01476 541080; fax 01476 541061; orders@gbs.tbs-ltd.co.uk

North American agent/distributor: National Book Network, 4501 Forbes Boulevard, Suite 200, Lanham, MD 20706
tel. 301 459 3366; fax 301 429 5746; www.nbnbooks.com

Australian agent/distributor: Pan Macmillan Australia, Level 18, St Martins Tower, 31 Market St, Sydney, NSW 2000
tel. 1300 135 113; fax 1300 135 103; customer.service@macmillan.com.au

New Zealand agent/distributor: David Bateman Ltd, 30 Tarndale Grove, Off Bush Road, Albany, Auckland
tel. (09) 415 7664; fax (09) 415 8892

A CIP catalogue record for this book is available from the British Library.

Publisher: Joanna Lorenz
Editor: Elizabeth Woodland
Production Controller: Darren Price
Senior Editor: Margaret Malone
Photographer: Nicki Dowey
Home Economist: Carol Tennant
Hand Model: Kirsty Fraser
Stylist: Helen Trent
Designer: Nigel Partridge
Additional Photography: Edward Allwright, Steve Baxter, Nicki Dowey, James Duncan, Gus Filgate, Ian Garlick,
Michelle Garrett, Amanda Heywood, Janine Hosegood, David Jordan, Dave King, Don Last, William Lingwood,
Thomas Odulate, Craig Robertson and Sam Stowell
Additional Recipes: Catherine Atkinson, Alex Barker, Angela Boggiano, Jacqueline Clark,
Carole Clements, Trish Davies, Roz Denny, Matthew Drennan, Joanna Farrow, Christine France, Yasuko Fukuoka,
Brian Glover, Nicola Graimes, Christine Ingram, Lucy Knox, Sue Maggs, Sally Mansfield, Maggie Mayhew, Norma Miller,
Sallie Morris, Jenni Shapter, Anne Sheasby, Hilaire Walden, Kate Whiteman, Elizabeth Wolf-Cohen and Jeni Wright

Previously published as part of a larger volume, *The Citrus Cookbook*

10 9 8 7 6 5 4 3 2 1

NOTES

Bracketed terms are intended for American readers.
For all recipes, quantities are given in both metric and imperial measures and, where appropriate,
measures are also given in standard cups and spoons. Follow one set, but not a mixture, because they are not interchangeable.
Standard spoon and cup measures are level. 1 tsp = 5ml, 1 tbsp = 15ml, 1 cup = 250ml/8fl oz
Australian standard tablespoons are 20ml. Australian readers should use 3 tsp in place of 1 tbsp
for measuring small quantities of gelatine, flour, salt, etc.
Medium (US large) eggs are used unless otherwise stated.
The very young, the elderly, pregnant women and those in ill-health or with a compromised immune system
are advised against consuming raw eggs or dishes and drinks containing raw eggs.

CONTENTS

INTRODUCTION

From their cultivation in China and India, thousands of years ago, citrus fruits have been highly valued by people all around the world. They have inspired much art and architecture, been a source of scientific fascination and study, and have constituted an important trade commodity. Not least, however, they offer something unique to food and drinks, be it the fresh taste of an orange or the bittersweet bite of a grapefruit.

The citrus family has grown rapidly over the last few decades, so that today varieties differing enormously in size, shape, colour and taste are grown worldwide in over 100 countries. Each fruit has something special to offer, whether it is the quality of the juice, the sweetness of the segments, the aromatic essential oils in the skin or the way in which even just a small quantity of grated peel or dried rind can add a burst of flavour to any number of savoury and sweet dishes.

All kinds of fruit

Though rare and exciting new varieties of citrus are constantly appearing, this introduction focuses on the most widely cultivated ones. There are the "oranges and lemons" of the nursery rhyme; grapefruit that appear in shades of white, pink and ruby; new varieties of citrus such as fragrant citron, used in Jewish festivals; and the ungainly looking but sweet-tasting Ugli fruit.

Modern cross-breeding has resulted in many successful and delicious new specimens though, sometimes, the original is still the best. From the early bitter orange, for instance, which grew wild in China thousands of years ago, there are now almost 50 different varieties growing today, including juicy, seedless sweet oranges as well as the bitter Seville (Temple) oranges. Despite this wide choice, Seville oranges are still considered by experts – and seasoned marmalade makers – to be the only orange to use for marmalade.

Above: Citrus medica*, citron, has been used in the Jewish festival of Sukkot or Tabernacles for centuries.*

First fruit

From its early history, citrus fruits have developed into an important source of trade throughout the world. Often initially viewed as marvellous botanical curiosities, scientific innovation has led to the breeding and exporting of many new varieties of citrus fruit.

In the ancient world, oranges and mandarins first grew in China, where the word "mandarin" also meant a powerful official. Traders carried fruit to India and Arabia, and on to Greece and the shores of the Mediterranean. The Golden Apples of the Hesperides, stolen by the Greek hero Heracles, may have been bitter oranges. Lemons and limes originally grew in India or Malaysia and, through trade, were introduced into Assyria. From there, the soldiers of Alexander the Great took them to Greece. In ancient Athens and Sparta, lemons were used as a flavouring for food, and for medicinal and cosmetic purposes. Roman gardeners planted orange groves in Italy and they may have taken them to Spain. Other historians believe that Muslim invaders

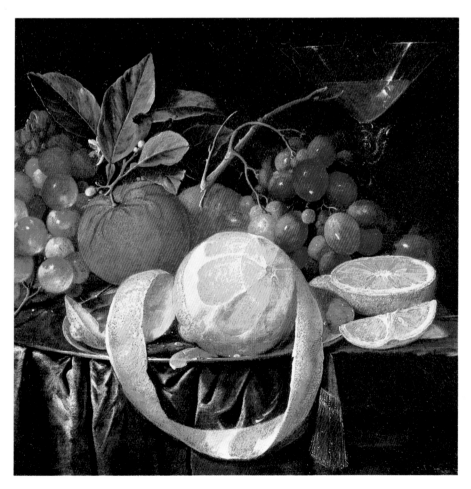

Left: Citrus fruit has long been a source of inspiration to artists, as shown in this still life of grapes, oranges and a lemon by J Gillemans (1618–75).

Above: Two well-dressed ladies buy sweet oranges from a street vendor, engraving by L Schiavonetti, 1794.

were responsible for first introducing them to Spain. Oranges were known as *narayam* or "perfume within" in India 3,000 years ago, and to the Arabs as *narandj.* The Italians softened it to *arancia*, and with a shift of sound, and because the medieval town of Orange was a centre for cultivation of the fruit, the French word became orange.

After the fall of the Roman Empire, the Arabs continued to cultivate oranges and lemons. The Jews also specialized in producing citrus fruit, and today many areas of citrus production were once places where Jews lived. Citron was used as a Jewish symbol on coins and gravestones and in synagogues. When the Jews were expelled from Spain and England, they went to live in northern and eastern Europe, returning to southern Italy, Spain and Sicily each year to buy a variety of citron – known as etrog in the Bible – to help them celebrate the Feast of Tabernacles or Sukkot. At the same time, Jewish merchants brought goods from the north and east, helping to establish trade routes in medieval Europe.

Right: Oranges are packed into crates for export in Andalucía, Spain 1888. Early on, merchants recognized the commercial value of citrus fruit.

Soldiers returned from the Crusades in Palestine via Italian ports, bringing oranges with them. One 11th-century pilgrim to the Holy Land found a fruit called "Adam's apple", a variety of pomelo. "Saracen" brides wore white orange blossoms in their hair as a symbol of innocence and fecundity – an orange tree can bear 3000–4000 oranges in a year. Centuries later, many brides in the Western world still feature orange blossoms in their headdress.

History and trade

In the 15th century, European explorers expanded their knowledge of the world, travelling to the Far East and to America. Christopher Columbus took all kinds of citrus seeds – bitter and sweet oranges, lemon, lime and citron – to Haiti on his second voyage in 1493. Fruit became an exciting commodity with its strong bright colours. In Italy, the Medici coat-of-arms showed five golden oranges. Sweet-smelling

pomanders, made from bitter oranges studded with cloves and herbs, were used by Cardinal Wolsey and others in Tudor England. The rich flavoured their food with bitter orange juice and aromatic citrus rind. In France, lemon juice made the lips red and the complexion pale.

By the 17th century, when "pretty, witty Nell Gwynne" sold sweet Portuguese oranges as an exotic snack in Drury Lane Theatre in London, orange marmalades and candied citrus fruits were incredibly popular. Unlike today, when the Seville orange season in Europe lasts a bare four weeks, it then extended from All Hallows Day (1 November) through to April. At that time, marmalade was a stiff candied paste that could be cut into squares as a sweetmeat.

Up until the 19th century most oranges were bitter, though the first sweet oranges were probably brought back to Europe by Vasco da Gama after his Cape of Good Hope voyage in 1498. A growing interest in science and a desire for sweeter, tastier fruit led to the rapid development of many hybrids and cross-breeds. Grapefruits and tangerines were crossed to produce varieties of tangelo, including minneolas and Ugli fruit. Sweet oranges and Mexican limes were crossed with the kumquat to produce orangequats and limequats.

Artists and botanical painters such as Jan Pauwel Gillemans the Elder recorded these strange new fruits in still-lifes while Giuseppe Arcimboldo produced extraordinary fruit portraits such as Winter, which shows an old bearded man sprouting leaves and lemons. Architects designed orangeries, extravagant houses in which these rare fruits were grown and the fashionable could walk. Henri IV of France may have erected the first orangery at the Tuileries to shelter the trees from frost, but it was his grandson Louis XIV, the Sun King, who built at Versailles the most magnificent orangery in Europe.

There his chief gardener, la Quintinie produced asparagus in January, strawberries for nine months a year and sweet-scented orange blossom.

A variety of uses

As citrus fruit ceased to be a rare commodity and became more widely accepted, horticulturalists and cooks sought ways to preserve the acid scent of citrus fruit. Distillation produced neroli, an essential oil used in perfume making (named after Anne Maria de la Tremoille, Princess of Nerole), and orange flower water. Bergamot oil was used to perfume the barley sugar made in the French town of Nancy, and also Earl Grey tea, named after a British prime minister in the early 1800s.

People long ago discovered that if you can eat a food, you can also turn it into alcohol. Dutch settlers in the Caribbean island of Curaçao began the tradition of flavouring white rum with the bitter peel of green oranges. This technique was eventually adopted by the French who are today famous for

Above: A view of the orangerie in Lord Burlington's garden, Chiswick, England, 18th century.

the orange-based liqueurs Cointreau and Grand Marnier. Elsewhere, lemons were used in Limoncello in Italy and Limonnaya vodka in Russia, and Mandarine Napoléon is said to have been the Emperor's favourite tipple.

An expanding market

During this period of discovery and growth, there was a constant exchange of varieties of new fruit between Europe and the New World. Oranges from Paraguay and the West Indies were exported to Europe. Dutch settlers planted orange and lemon trees in South Africa. In 1828, the French count Odette Phillippe introduced the grapefruit into Florida, and the state started on its journey to becoming the world's largest producer of grapefruit. In the southern hemisphere, oranges, limes and lemons reached Australia by the end of the 18th century.

At this time doctors realized that citrus juice could prevent scurvy, and British sailors were nicknamed "limeys" by the Americans. After a certain number of days at sea, British sailors were issued with lime juice, liberally mixed with rum, to prevent scurvy, a killing disease. A whole area of London became known as Limehouse, after the great warehouses of limes stored there.

Imports of citrus continued to grow in number of variety and frequency: loose-skinned mandarins, for instance, were introduced to Europe and America in the 19th century. Children found mandarins in the toes of their Christmas stockings, since this fruit came into season around Christmas in Europe, and street-sellers cried, "Who will buy my sweet oranges?"

The modern era has seen a whole new range of fruit juices and fruit products in the shops. The development of sweet oranges from the original bitter oranges means that fruit juice has become an increasingly popular drink. Florida is famous for its oranges and grapefruits and most of the fruit grown there is turned into juice: its people are among the highest consumers of juice

Below: Every part of the Seville orange is highly valued, including the leaves, blossoms and fruit. Drawing from Kew Gardens Library, 19th century.

in the world. Fruit-growing is a major industry in the USA and Brazil, and production of oranges and lemons is a vital part of some countries' GNP. Citric acid is used as a flavouring in a huge variety of commercially produced foods and drinks. Scientists strive to synthesize the flavour for the food industry, but nothing can compare with the real thing.

Cooking with citrus

Virtually every cuisine is touched by the refreshing zesty tang of citrus. Oranges still claim the title of the world's favourite citrus fruit, while lemons and limes provide the undertones in hundreds of dishes. Every country has its own way of preparing citrus fruit. In Morocco, cooks store their harvest of lemons by preserving them with a generous amount of salt and water; in Italy, lemons flavour anything from ice cream to pasta sauces. Greek cuisine is liberally laced with lemons, from egg-and-lemon *avgolemono* to *limonato*, a rich pot-roast of beef flavoured with lemons. Sephardic Jews have many recipes for orange cakes and preserves. Seville orange marmalade is a British breakfast classic.

As well as the juice from the fruit, everything else can be used – flowers, leaves and rinds. The blossoms that form on trees of the bitter or Seville orange are turned into intensively perfumed orange flower or orange blossom water, particularly in the Middle East.

The age-old techniques of preserving the rinds by candying and caramelizing are perfect for decorating cakes and desserts, and a sliver of lemon, orange or lime peel tied up with the herbs that make a bouquet garni, gives it that something extra special.

Limes, although a relatively recent introduction to the West, have been used extensively in Asian cuisines for many centuries, their subtle fragrance enhancing curries, noodle and rice dishes, pickles and chutneys. In Peru, lime juice is used in the classic dish *ceviche*, where it "cooks" raw white fish without heat.

Above: Loading citrus at San Antonio, Paraguay, 1891.

Just juice?

Citrus fruit not only improves the flavour of food, it also nourishes. Nutritional values vary, so it is worth getting to know all the members of this diverse family of fruit. Choosing the best fruit can be difficult. An orange or lemon that feels heavy in the hand may indicate that it bears the maximum amount of juice. However, the Ugli fruit has a large central core, which makes it feel light for its size. Look out for organic fruit and try to use unwaxed fruit in recipes involving the zest.

Apart from vitamin C, present in all types, oranges contain vitamin A and many minerals. Lemons are an excellent source of bioflavonoids, which are a good antioxidant, cleansing the blood, and the juice is a well-known antiseptic, especially good for sore throats. Pink grapefruit contains an amazing five times the amount of vitamin A present in its white relative.

After reading all about this most fascinating family of fruit, turn to the wonderful collection of recipes. They are full of flavour and colour, and prove just how versatile citrus fruit can be. All that flavour is but a squeeze away.

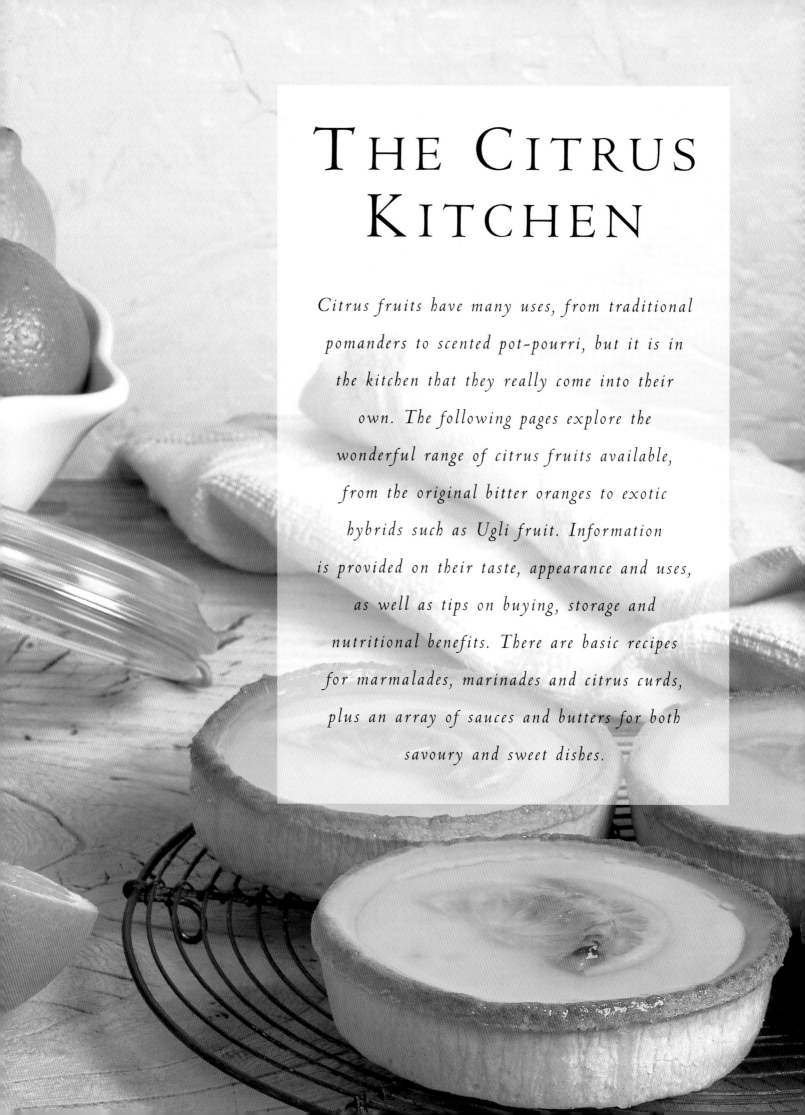

THE CITRUS KITCHEN

Citrus fruits have many uses, from traditional pomanders to scented pot-pourri, but it is in the kitchen that they really come into their own. The following pages explore the wonderful range of citrus fruits available, from the original bitter oranges to exotic hybrids such as Ugli fruit. Information is provided on their taste, appearance and uses, as well as tips on buying, storage and nutritional benefits. There are basic recipes for marmalades, marinades and citrus curds, plus an array of sauces and butters for both savoury and sweet dishes.

ORANGES

Arguably the world's favourite citrus fruit, if not *the* favourite of all fruit, oranges are not always orange. They can be green, yellow or dappled with red. There are hundreds of varieties, ranging from the size of a tennis ball to almost football-size proportions. Some have honey-sweet flesh, while others are so bitter as to be quite inedible.

All citrus peel contains essential oils, and peel from the orange is used in perfume-making and cosmetics, as well as in cooking. Depending on the variety, oranges grow well in tropical, semi-tropical and sub-tropical regions. They ripen on the tree, and do not continue to ripen after picking, so have excellent keeping qualities.

History

The bitter orange probably originated around China and India, and the fruit has been grown in southern China for thousands of years. There is no record of the Romans having cultivated oranges, and it wasn't until around the middle of the 15th century that their cultivation reached the Mediterranean, having first travelled across the Middle East with Arab traders who brought the fruit across from China.

The name orange comes from the ancient Indian word *narayam*. Arabs called the fruit *narandj* and in Italy the word lost its initial vowel and became *arancia*. It is thought that, during medieval times in France, the fruit acquired the name by which it is most widely known today – taking the name of the town of Orange, where there was a large trade in the fruit. Like other commodities introduced by the Arabs into Europe, such as silks, sugar and spices, oranges were a rarity and were synonymous with wealth (the Medici family in Italy chose five oranges as their coat of arms). However, these early cultivars were far too bitter – and too precious – to eat raw, so they were made into preserves, and prized for their perfumed flowers.

The Portuguese, in particular, played a large part in cultivating the bitter orange, patiently developing new varieties. We have them to thank for most of the sweet oranges we eat today, which have their origin in trees that Portuguese farmers imported from China in the middle of the 17th century. These early varieties, which we would probably still consider to be quite bitter, became a novelty theatre snack and one that only the rich could afford.

Oranges do not flourish in cold climates, but this did not deter early 19th-century British gardeners, who were very taken with the exotic fruit. They eagerly adopted the Italian practice of cultivating the fruit in large glasshouses, which could be heated in the winter, and the orangery – the forerunner of the greenhouse – became a much sought-after status symbol.

Christopher Columbus is credited with introducing the orange to America. There is evidence that they were first cultivated in Florida in the 16th century, and introduced to California by Spanish missionaries about two hundred years later. The orange-growing industry became solidly established towards the end of the 19th century and the United States now grows more oranges than any other type of fruit; about one-sixth of the world's supply. Today, oranges are produced on a global scale: China, Spain, Greece, Italy, Morocco, the USA, Turkey, Israel, Australia and South Africa are the main producers.

Orange flower water

Also known as orange blossom water, this is distilled from the waxy white, star-shaped blossoms that appear before the citrus tree bears fruit. It will enhance the taste of any citrus fruit, especially oranges, and is wonderful in ice creams and fruit salads, jellies (flavoured gelatine) and sorbets (sherbets). Some Middle Eastern salads are dressed with a sprinkling of orange flower water, which lends them a fresh fragrant air.

Above: Valencia are the world's most popular variety of orange.

Varieties

Oranges fall into two principal groups: sweet oranges, which can be eaten raw, and bitter oranges, which cannot.

Sweet oranges, *Citrus sinensis*

Blond or common oranges These are pale-skinned winter varieties like Jaffa or Shamouti (the easiest oranges to peel). A variety called Pineapple is grown in Florida, mainly for its juice as it can be rather pippy, and Natal comes from Brazil. Valencia is the world's favourite eating orange and is grown in all the orange-producing countries: it was sent in the 1860s from the Azores islands, near Portugal, to Thomas Rivers of Hertfordshire, Great Britain, who cultivated it for the orangeries in grand houses. It was originally called Rivers Late, but was renamed Valencia Late in 1887, not because it had any real Spanish connections, but because an expert from Spain thought it was similar to an orange grown in Valencia. The fruits are medium to large, with reasonably thin rind, which is finely marked. Valencias are easy to peel, and have juicy flesh.

Blood or pigmented oranges If it's colour you are after, these are the oranges to use, especially for sorbets (sherbets) and similar iced desserts. With names such as Sanguina, Sanguigna and Sanguine, derived from *sanguis*, the Latin word for blood, they have red-tinged skin and golden or ruby red flesh. The red pigment develops naturally when the trees grow where the temperature at night is low; cold storage can also affect a similar change in the fruit's colour.

Bittersweet blood oranges originated in either Malta or Sicily, and the fruit is a key ingredient in the sauce Maltaise, an orange-flavoured mayonnaise, which takes its name from the island's juicy but sour variety of blood orange. Moro is a variety grown mainly in Italy, particularly on the island of Sicily.

Above: Seedless navel oranges have very sweet juicy flesh.

Navel oranges These take their name from the small orange that grows inside the apex of the main fruit, a bit like a belly button. The navel, which is the earliest orange to mature, is seedless, sweet and juicy and great for eating in the hand. The most popular navel varieties are the Washington or Bahia navel, Cara Cara, and Lane Late from Australia, or its renamed Spanish version, Navelate. The thick skin is good for making candied peel.

Sugar or acidless oranges These varieties are not cultivated on a vast scale and have a very low acid content and a bland, rather insipid flavour. They are seldom exported, but are more usually grown for local consumption. In the countries where they grow – mainly the Mediterranean region and some parts of South America – they go by a range of different names, such as Lima (Brazil), Dolce (Italy) and Sucreña (Spain).

Above: Blood oranges

Left: Sweet oranges, Citrus sinensis

Bitter oranges, *Citrus aurantium*

These were the first variety of oranges. They originated in India and China and gradually spread through Asia to Europe and North Africa, arriving eventually in the Iberian peninsula, from where they were said to be introduced to the New World by Christopher Columbus.

Seville oranges – known as Bigarade in France or Temple in the USA – taste bitter owing to a compound called neohesperidin. You can't eat them raw, but they are ideal for use in marmalade. In industry, they feature in liqueurs and some soft drinks, and the flowers

from special varieties called *bouquetiers* are used to make oil of neroli, which is used in perfumery. In Europe, Sevilles make a fleeting appearance for a couple of weeks in January, but they freeze well, as does their juice, so if you're not up to making marmalade then and you

have enough freezer space, you can store them and make marmalade when you feel like it. The rind is good dried.

Seville oranges are also grown in California and Arizona, purely for their decorative shade on streets, and Japan and China also produce small numbers of their own bitter orange.

Nutrition

Packed with vitamin C, which is highest at the start of the season in winter, oranges are also a source of vitamin A and folic acid and the minerals calcium, potassium and phosphorus. The white pith contains pectin, which, as well as acting as a setting agent for marmalade, helps to lower blood cholesterol levels, and also bioflavonoids, which keep your gums and blood healthy.

Buying and storing

Oranges crop at different times of the year, depending on the variety and, as they are grown worldwide, climate dictates when that will be. You'll always be able to buy oranges all year round, but winter is the optimum time. Cup a fruit in your hand and if it feels heavy, the chances are that it will be full of juice. The skin should be taut and blemish-free. Although annoying, pips (seeds) are not a sign of inferior quality; their presence

Left: Bitter Seville oranges

Above: Seville oranges are considered by many to be the best type for making orange marmalade.

just depends on the variety. And, as a bowl of bright oranges is a welcome sight during any monochrome winter, it's good to know that they'll keep for two weeks in the refrigerator. The juice and pared or grated rind can be frozen.

Serving ideas

The simplest way to enjoy an orange is to cut it into quarters and use your teeth to extract the flesh. A less messy method is to separate the segments and serve them just as they are or moistened with freshly squeezed orange juice. The fruit makes an excellent flavouring for cakes, particularly rich fruit cakes and biscuits (cookies). Segments and slices are decorative as well as delicious, and look good in home-made fruit jellies, or as a caramelized topping for an orange flan. Oranges make very good sorbets (sherbets), ice creams and savoury or sweet sauces, especially when teamed with brandy or an orange liqueur as in the sauce for crêpes Suzette.

Oranges are equally at home in a savoury setting. Orange rind is used to flavour stews in both the French and Chinese traditions, while segments are famously used in the inimitable *canard à l'orange*. Juice and rind are excellent

partners in marinades, stuffings or sauces for meat, poultry and fish, and make a refreshing salad dressing, while segments are classically combined with beetroot (beet) and chicory (Belgian endive). The juice and rind perk up mild, creamy cheeses and complement sweet red onions and glazed carrots.

Commercial uses

Oranges are highly versatile so it is no surprise that they are used in many products, ranging from freshly squeezed orange juice to traditional marmalades.

Marmalades

These days, commercial marmalades may contain every type of citrus fruit, with ginger, vanilla and other spices joining spirits, such as brandy and whisky, to create exciting new flavours. Given the choice, however, many people will still plump for a traditional recipe, and thick-cut Seville orange is one of the best.

Liqueurs and cordials

Curaçao Dutch settlers on the Caribbean island of Curaçao first made this white rum-based liqueur. It is flavoured with bitter green oranges (not a bitter variety, just unripened). Although it is usually known by the name of its island home, versions of this liqueur are also made in many other countries, under a variety of names, and brandy is often used as a base instead of rum. Triple Sec is another name for Curaçao, although *sec*, a French word meaning dry, is a bit of a misnomer, as Triple Sec is sweet.

Curaçao is always flavoured with oranges, but comes in a variety of colours for novelty value – red, yellow, blue and vivid green – although the clear type is always Triple Sec.

Cointreau Cointreau is a Curaçao with a brandy base. Launched in 1849 by the brothers Edouard and Adolphe Cointreau, it was originally known as Triple Sec White Curaçao. However, at that time other branded Curaçaos were being sold as Triple Sec, so it seemed good business sense

to make theirs eponymous. It is very sweet and made with a blend of the Caribbean bitter green oranges and sweeter varieties from France.

Grand Marnier This branded Curaçao was devised in 1880 by Louis-Alexandre Marnier, who blended unripened oranges with the finest cognac, which was then aged in barrels. This aging gives it a superior taste to that of other Curaçaos. Grand Marnier has a highly refined, mellow flavour and the sweetness is tempered by the Cognac.

Aurum The name of this brandy-based Italian liqueur hints at gold, which it may once have contained. Today, however, the glorious golden colour is the result of a mixture of infused orange peel and whole oranges, enhanced by the addition of saffron.

Below: Grand Marnier is made from bitter green oranges and fine Cognac. Louis-Alexander Marnier first hit upon the idea for the drink after tasting bitter oranges in Haiti in 1880.

LEMONS

Where would we be without the lemon? We would have nothing to squeeze over our fish; our avocados and artichokes would turn brown; and we would be denied lemon curd and lemon meringue pie. With their wonderful, fresh, tart flavour, lemons are not only an excellent single flavouring in their own right, but also enhance the flavour of a vast range of other ingredients.

Lemons thrive in all climates, but most are grown in sub-tropical regions, as the humidity in hotter countries encourages pests and diseases. Unlike other citrus fruits, which usually flower once a year, lemon trees blossom several times during the season and you'll find fruit of various ages on the tree at the same time. Lemons do not ripen once they have been picked and will last for up to two weeks.

History

The familiar Italian or Mediterranean lemon is actually a cross between a citron, the Indian lime, and another (as yet unidentified) member of the citrus family. It is believed to have originated in the Punjab region of India and Pakistan, and may also have been cultivated in the Middle East. Unusually,

Below: Smooth-skinned lemons are best for juicing.

there is no Latin word for lemon, although there is some evidence that the Romans used the lemon as a condiment, in medicine and for decoration. They may also have grown the fruit themselves.

It was the Arabs who introduced lemons to Europe in the 4th century AD. They were soon extensively cultivated in Spain, Sicily and across the Mediterranean in North Africa. Lemons were also introduced into China – the Chinese name for lemon is *li ming*. The name lemon is derived from Persian via both Arabic and French.

Lemons were scarce in Northern Europe during the Middle Ages and were a luxury even for the wealthy.

Christopher Columbus took seeds to the New World in 1493, where lemons were hitherto unknown. The Portuguese introduced the fruit to Brazil, and the Brazilians, in turn, took it to Australia, where the first trees

Above: These Argentinian Eureka lemons are waxed, enhancing their golden colour.

were planted in 1788. Scurvy was rife on these early colonist ships, but it wasn't until the end of the 18th century that it was finally realized that the disease, caused by a deficiency of vitamin C, could be cured by eating citrus fruit. If only the sailors had known that the solution to their swollen gums and suppurating skin lay in the cargo they were carrying.

Varieties

Distinguishing between varieties of lemons can be extremely tricky. There is less difference between the types than is the case with oranges or mandarins, and the problem is further exacerbated by the fact that the shape of a lemon and the thickness of its skin varies, depending on the time of year. Their skin and pith can be thick or thin, the skin itself can be smooth or bumpy, and the juice mouth-puckering to almost sweet.

Eureka Although it was originally cultivated in Europe, and is still commonly grown in Spain, this variety is today the favourite of countries such as Australia, South Africa, Argentina and Israel. Fairly

Right: These fruit are Jambhiri lemons, though varietal names are rarely given in stores.

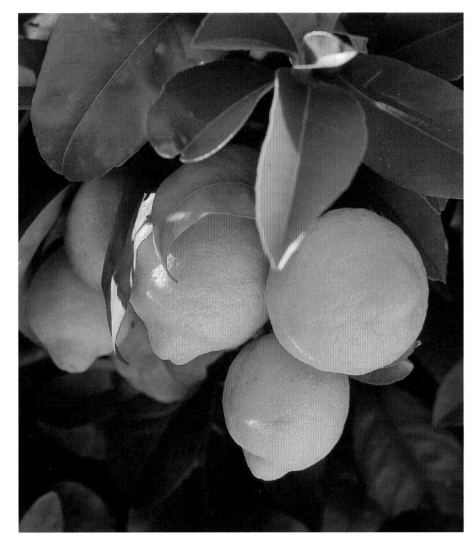

thin-skinned and very juicy, it is also a popular variety in California, where it was introduced from Sicily in 1858.

Femminello Commune This variety comprises around three-quarters of the Italian lemon crop, but is also grown in Argentina and Turkey. In Italy, it crops four times a year and each season's crop has a different name: Primofiori (September–November), Limoni (December–May), Bianchetti (April–June), and Verdilli (June–August). Femminello Commune lemons have medium skin and pith, but a lower than average juice content.

Lisbon As the name suggests, this was originally a Portuguese lemon variety, but it was developed in Australia, where it continues to be grown successfully. Lisbon lemons are also grown in California and South America. The juicy fruits are on the large side, with fairly thin, slightly rough rind. They crop during the winter and into early spring.

Fino or Primofiori A Spanish variety, this smooth-skinned lemon is relatively small, and can be rounded or oval in shape. In the northern hemisphere, it crops between October and February.

Verna This fruit accounts for about 60 per cent of the Spanish summer crop and has a rough, rather thick rind.

Above: Pale-skinned, unwaxed Italian Primofiori lemons.

Nutrition

As well as the vital vitamin C, lemons are an excellent source of bioflavonoids, which have important antioxidant properties that help maintain the immune system and protect against disease, including some forms of cancer. They also contain small amounts of the minerals potassium, calcium and phosphorus. A famous antiseptic, lemon juice soothes sore throats, especially when combined with a spoonful of honey in a warm drink – with or without a tot of whisky. It is also believed that lemons can ease rheumatism.

Lemon lore
• When rubbed on the hands, lemon juice will rid them of lingering fishy smells and other cooking odours.
• A glass of water spiked with lemon juice can aid digestion and help cleanse the system.
• If in need of something acidic to prevent browning (such as cut apples), lemon juice is perfect.

Left: Growers know lemons by the shape of their stalk and pointed end, which vary – albeit subtly – between varieties.

It is the skin of the lemon that holds the really powerful flavouring ingredient, however. If you rub a lump of sugar over the surface of a lemon it will soak up the aromatic oil. Use the sugar in a dessert sauce or cocktail, and it will add a subtle citrus flavour. Grated or pared lemon rind tastes wonderful in cakes, desserts and even savoury dishes, such as beef, lamb, pork or

Buying and storing

Growers talk of nipples (the stalk end) and necks (where the lemon elongates) but, apart from minor differences in these two areas, the only feature that distinguishes one lemon from another at the market is whether the skin is rough or smooth. Lemons are seldom, if ever, labelled as to variety. The most you can hope for is a clue to the country of origin so, until you take the fruit home and cut it open, you cannot be sure whether what you have chosen is juicy or not, or if it will have thin skin and pith, or thick skin with sometimes as much as 1cm/½in of pith.

Sprightly, taut skin is what you are looking for with a good, clear, bright yellow colour. Lemons gradually become paler and less juicy as they ripen.

Where possible, always buy unwaxed lemons, sometimes also described as untreated, or organic lemons. The wax (diphenyl, an ethylene gas) works rather like shoe polish in that it makes the fruit shine and helps preserve it. It is considered to be harmless to health, but if you are intending to use the lemon rind, either by grating or paring it, thoroughly scrub a waxed lemon before using. This will also remove any pesticide residue.

When you buy a bag of lemons off the supermarket shelf use them as soon after purchase as possible. If stored in the refrigerator, they will be fine for up to two weeks; at room temperature they will keep for slightly less. However, the longer you leave them, the more their nutritional value will fade.

Serving ideas

All dishes, both sweet and savoury, benefit from the distinctive tang of this well-loved citrus fruit. It is seldom served solo, except when preserved or transformed into lemonade, but rather it is used primarily to enhance or flavour other foods.

Lemon juice will tenderize meat in a marinade, give fresh cream a soured taste, and prevent fruit and vegetables – especially apples, celeriac, artichokes, avocados and potatoes – from oxidizing and browning. It also makes a great marinade for both fish and shellfish, but do not marinate for more than an hour or the juice will start to "cook" or denature the protein. The juice can feature as the principal flavouring in such dishes as lemon mousse, sorbet (sherbet) or cheesecake or as a complementary flavour, for example, in a lemon mayonnaise or cake frosting.

Iced lemon tea

Although black tea tastes great hot with a slice of lemon, it is also very good chilled, especially on a hot, humid afternoon.

1 Mix the juice of 2 lemons with 1.75 litres/3 pints/7½ cups cold water in a large jug or pitcher. Add 3–4 Earl Grey or Lapsang Souchong tea bags and 6–8 fresh mint leaves.

2 Add about 90ml/6 tbsp sugar to the juice, to sweeten, stirring well. Remember that chilling will blunt the sweetness somewhat.

3 Cover tightly and chill for at least 8 hours to allow the flavours to develop. Strain into glasses and decorate with fresh lemon slices and mint leaves.

chicken casseroles. When paring or grating lemons, take care not to include any of the pith, which is unpleasantly bitter. Where the pith is useful is in helping jam to set, since it contains a lot of pectin, as do the pips (seeds).

Preserved lemons feature in both sweet and savoury recipes. Sliced or quartered lemons, preserved in salt and stored in olive oil are widely used in North African cooking, especially in chicken and fish dishes. Candied lemon slices or half slices may be used to decorate creamy desserts and tarts.

Slices or wedges of lemon are classic garnishes for hot and cold fish and shellfish dishes. They are also natural partners for chicken and veal and the favourite decoration for cocktails. Finely grated lemon rind may be sprinkled over both sweet and savoury dishes and, combined with finely chopped flat leaf parsley and garlic cloves, it forms an Italian garnish called *gremolata*.

Commercial uses

By far, the most felicitious uses of lemon have been in drinks, spirits and liqueurs, but pre-squeezed lemon juice and lemon curd are also available for use in cooking. For light refreshment,

choose from lemon tea, lemon cordial or traditional, old-fashioned lemonade, and use lemon liqueurs to enliven cocktails or serve with coffee after dinner.

Lemon drinks

Limoncello This Italian lemon liqueur is made from a base alcohol steeped with lemon rind and sugar. Serve added to a fruit salad or drizzle over ice cream.

Limonnaya Fruit flavourings are quite common for vodka. Limonnaya is a leading lemon-flavoured brand.

Liquore al limone or Cedro This sticky, sweet liqueur is made from the peel of the lemons that grow in profusion around the Amalfi coast in south-west Italy. Almost every delicatessen in the region sells a home-made version of this opaque yellow drink, whose sweetness is toned down by the tangy citrus fruit. It should be served ice-cold straight from the refrigerator or freezer and makes a refreshing aperitif or digestif.

Lemon barley water A traditional English cordial, this is made

from ground barley, water, lemon rind and juice, sweetened with sugar or honey. It is not so popular as it once was, but remains a good choice at picnics or after playing sport.

Lemon cordial In Britain, the name is given to a wide range of concentrated lemon drinks that are mixed with water. Some are full of sugar or artificial sweeteners, but better quality cordials are useful for making long, cold drinks for lazy summer afternoons. American cordials are alcoholic.

Below: Lemon products include fizzy soft drinks, pre-squeezed lemon juice and herbal tea bags.

Right: Limonnaya, a popular brand of lemon-flavoured Russian vodka

Far right: Liquore al limone

LIMES

Of the true members of the citrus family, limes are the smallest of the fruits. Their thin, bright green skin has an exquisite perfume, and the juice has a clean, sharp taste. Limes grow in tropical regions and need heat and high humidity if they are to thrive, although they do well in the dry heat of Egypt, where the crop outdoes that of the lemon. In cooking, lime plays a central role in the cuisines of Thailand and all of South-east Asia, as well as in the Caribbean, Mexico and south America.

History

Although India is often cited as the original home of the lime, historical data is scanty and each variety needs to be looked at independently. Limes seem to have been missing from both the Greek and the Roman cuisines and, when they were mentioned in early Arabic texts, a single word – *limah* – was used for both lemons and limes. One possible reason for this is that when limes are left to ripen fully on the tree, their skins turn a sunny yellow, giving them the appearance of lemons.

Limes grow well in the Caribbean, and it was from there that British sailors stocked up with the fruit as protection against scurvy. This led to the British being known as "limeys", and the area of London's docklands where the cargo was stored was named Limehouse.

Varieties

The glossy green fruit we collectively know as limes are so different from one another that they are actually classified as separate species. Most limes are picked before they are fully mature and still green.

Acid or sour limes

West Indian, Mexican or Key lime, *Citrus aurantifolia* Extreme heat is essential if this type of lime is to flourish, and it is not often found for sale in Europe. Originally from Malaysia, it is now grown in Mexico, the Caribbean (where it is used to make lime cordial), Brazil, Peru, India, Iran and Egypt. Traditionally used for Key lime pie, this variety now accounts for only a tiny proportion of the crop in Florida. Small and thin-skinned, with a powerfully scented rind and yellow flesh, it is full of pips (seeds) and very juicy.

Tahitian or Persian lime, *Citrus latifolia*
This is the lime you are most likely to buy in Europe, imported mainly from Mexico, Florida and Brazil. It has a complicated history: it is thought to have originated in Asia and made its way to the Americas via Persia, the Mediterranean, Australia and Tahiti, reaching California in the latter half of the 19th century. It is no longer grown in either Tahiti or Iran. In America it is known as the Bearrs lime. Thin-skinned,

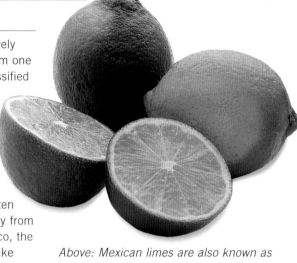

Above: Mexican limes are also known as West Indian or Key limes.

juicy and not so highly perfumed as the Key lime, it has yellowish-green flesh with no pips.

Makrut or Kaffir lime, *Citrus hystrix*
Grown on a small scale in Asia from Sri Lanka to the Philippines, this lime has extremely knobbly skin. The flesh inside is bitter, with lots of seeds and virtually no juice. The rind, however, is valued for its pungent fragrance. It is often grated and used in soups and salads.

Kaffir lime leaves are increasingly available, and are great in soups and noodle dishes. Their real name, Makrut, is seen by some to be more politically correct: Kaffir is an Arabic word for infidel, and in certain countries, notably South Africa, it is an offensive – and illegal – term of address.

Kalamansi or Musk lime, *Citrus mitis var. microcarpa* The flesh of this round, thin-skinned citrus fruit is bright yellow and full of flavour. Its alternative name – musk lime – refers to the flavour of the juice, which is less tart than that of most other limes and tastes musky. The kalamansi is native to the Philippines, but it is used throughout South-east Asia. It is the perfect partner for highly spiced chilli dishes. A popular drink is made from the sweetened juice.

Sweet or acidless limes

Australian wild limes *Microcitrus australasica* Fingerlimes, as these limes are known because of their shape, are wild fruit, native to Queensland and

Left: Tahitian lime blossom

northern New South Wales. They are cylindrical, 10cm/4in long and may be green, red, yellow, purple or black. They are mildly acidic and are seldom seen outside Australia. Other species of wild lime in that country include *Microcitrus australis*, a round fruit with thick skin that is good for candying.

Indian or Palestine lime, *Citrus limettioides* This lime is sweeter than other varieties and has a fairly bland flavour. It grows in India, Central and South America, and the Middle East. It is pale yellow when immature, ripening to orange. The flesh is very juicy, with few pips (seeds). You are unlikely to find it outside its growing areas.

Nutrition

Like lemons, limes are a rich source of vitamin C, and also contain potassium, calcium and phosphorus.

Buying and storing

Look for smooth, unblemished skins and fruit that feels a good weight for its size. Limes don't last as long as lemons and once a telltale browning appears around the ends, they should be thrown away. They look very pretty piled up in a bowl, but check the ones on the bottom as they will be susceptible to mould. It is better to keep them in the refrigerator, where they will last for up to one week.

Left: Makrut limes are not eaten raw or cooked, but the finely grated rind and the shredded leaves are widely used for flavouring in much Asian cooking.

Look for fresh and dried makrut or kaffir lime leaves at Asian and Indian stores and supermarkets.

Serving ideas

The most celebrated use for limes is in cocktails and drinks, such as margaritas and daiquiris. In cooking, Key lime pie from Florida, which is similar to a lemon meringue pie, but with a lime-flavoured filling, is perhaps the most famous dish. The meringue is sometimes omitted in favour of a cream topping. Grated lime

Above: Indian limes are sweeter and milder-tasting than other varieties.

rind and freshly squeezed juice flavour many iced desserts, and marmalade benefits from their pungent flavour.

In the Middle East, limes are dried and added to stews. In India, they are made into pickles and chutneys. Makrut or kaffir lime leaves are used in much the same way as bay leaves. A couple, torn or left whole, stirred into a Thai dish completes its flavour. In the classic South American dish of ceviche, chunks of raw white fish are marinated in lime juice. This changes or denatures the fish protein, so that it "cooks", turns opaque and tastes delicious.

A few pared strips of lime rind will perfume caster (superfine) sugar, and a little juice sprinkled over tropical fruit makes a fresh-tasting dessert.

Limes can be used as a substitute for lemons, but they have a sharper tang, so you will need fewer of them.

Commercial uses

The best-known lime product is cordial, but limes are also used in many pickles, chutneys and marmalades.

Lime cordial This lime concentrate makes a refreshing non-alcohoic drink with sparkling mineral water, though it is also essential in some classic cocktails.

MANDARINS

Strictly speaking, there is no such fruit as a mandarin. It is simply the umbrella name for a large group of citrus fruits, which includes the satsuma, tangelo, clementine and minneola. To further complicate the issue, the names are sometimes switched around so that the group is also designated as tangerine as well as mandarin. Furthermore, new hybrids are being developed.

All members of this extended family are smaller than the orange, have sweet and fragrant flesh, with a flavour that is distinctively different from that of the orange. They are also all characterized by their loose, sometimes puffy skins, which make them easy to peel. Some varieties are seedless, which makes them especially popular with children. There can be surprising differences between the various types: the satsuma, for instance, thrives in areas of the world that have cold winters, such as South America, New Zealand and its native Japan, while the clementine, which originated in Algeria, grows best in a Mediterranean climate.

History

The fruit is thought to have originated in China or India. Certainly, the Chinese have grown mandarins for many thousands of years – the earliest reference dates back to the

Above: Ripe Citrus reticulata *or common mandarin*

12th century BC. The name mandarin arrived some four hundred years later, a corruption of a Malay word derived from the Sanskrit *mantrin*, meaning counsellor, probably as a reference to the saffron-coloured robes worn by these Chinese court officials. By the beginning of the 10th century AD, Japan was also a prolific grower, but it wasn't until 1805 that the fruit was imported to England by Sir Abraham Hume, and from

there sent on to Malta and Italy. A further seventy years passed before the mandarin reached the United States, where large crops are now produced in the western and southern states. Once popularly known as "easy peelers" in Europe, mandarins are now correctly known by their varietal names.

Varieties

Part of the huge family of citrus fruits, there are many varieties.

Common mandarin, *Citrus reticulata*
Fruits in this group are the least easy to peel, as the skin clings more tightly to the segments, and

Left: Clementines

Mediterranean mandarin, *Citrus deliciosa* This variety was introduced to the sunny climes of the Mediterranean in 1805 via a journey that included England, Malta and Italy. This fruit is today primarily grown for use in the perfume and cosmetics industry, and to flavour soft drinks.

King mandarin, *Citrus nobilis* There are two varieties of this species. The first is the yellow king, which is large and round, closely resembling an orange in appearance, although the skin is rather more knobbly. This came originally from Vietnam and Cambodia, and was sent to California in 1880, although it is now grown almost exclusively in South-east Asia. The second variety is the kunenbo from Japan, which is smaller, with a smoother skin.

Mandarin hybrids

Calamondin, *Citrus mitis* This hybrid originated in the Philippines, and is thought to be a cross between a sour, loose-skinned mandarin and a kumquat. It is closely related to the kalamansi or musk lime. Calamondins are not eaten whole (as they are too acidic), instead the juice is used to flavour food, such as soups and stews.

Above: Satsumas have a refreshing flavour and are relatively easy to peel.

the clementine is a typical example. Once thought to be a cross between the Mediterranean mandarin and an inedible orange, the clementine is now believed to be a Chinese mandarin. It was named after a French missionary, Father Rodier, who found the fruit growing in his Algerian garden in 1902. It is now grown in Spain, Italy, South Africa and South America.

Satsuma or Unshiu mikan, *Citrus unshiu* This popular variety, with its sweet but tangy flavour, comes from an area that is now called Kagoshima in western Japan, but was formerly known as Satsuma. The fruit was given its name in 1878 by the wife of General Van Valkenberg, the United States Minister to Japan. It is now grown mostly in China and Korea, with smaller crops in Japan and Spain. It is also grown in Turkey, New Zealand, South America and California and Louisiana in the USA.

Satsumas are seedless and ideally suited to canning. Almost the entire Japanese crop is purchased every year for canning, and the fresh fruit is rarely available. It is generally marketed under the generic name of mandarin.

Right: Calamondin

Above: Minneola

Ortanique Known in South Africa as a tambor, this is actually a tangor, which is a cross between a mandarin and an orange. The skin is tough and not very easy to peel, but it is worth persevering with, for the flesh is juicy and sweet.

Minneola This bright orange fruit is the result of crossing a Duncan grapefruit with a Dancy tangerine, a hybrid that is known as a tangelo. The grapefruit lends the fruit tartness and the tangerine sweetness. It is seedless, with juicy, sweet flesh.

Below: Dried mandarin peel

Nutrition

In common with oranges, lemons and limes, all mandarins and their hybrids yield vitamin C, as well as smaller amounts of the essential minerals potassium, calcium and phosphorus.

Buying and storing

Mandarins look like little flattened oranges. Some varieties have quite loose, puffy skins, but this isn't an indication of quality; rather a characteristic of the type. Again, it's the weight in your hand that signifies a juicy fruit. If buying pre-packed fruit, check that there isn't a mouldy one lurking in the bottom, as this will quickly taint all the others. Keep mandarins in the refrigerator for up to one week, but bring them to room temperature first if eating fresh, so that the full flavour can reassert itself.

Serving ideas

With aromatic skins and juicy segments that virtually separate themselves, mandarins are ideal for eating in the hand. They taste best fresh, as cooking diminishes their delicate, sweet flavour. Use them in the same ways you would oranges. The rind is often soft, but can be grated. It can also be cut into strips and dried in a low oven, then used as part of a bouquet garni or to flavour a rich casserole, stew or soup. Mandarin segments taste delicious as part of a fruit platter, in a mixed fruit salad, caramelized or dipped in melted chocolate. The shells make pretty containers for ice cream or sorbets (sherbets). Mixed with Chinese five-spice powder, or star anise, ginger and soy sauce, the freshly squeezed juice makes a wonderful marinade for chicken, duck or pork.

Commercial uses

Apart from the canning industry, the main commercial products are liqueurs.
Van der Hum This is South Africa's version of Curaçao, made by steeping the local mandarins or *naartjies* as they are known, in brandy. Nutmeg is often added as a flavouring, as are other spices or aromatic herbs.
Mandarine Napoléon This is also a type of Curaçao, made with the skins of mandarins, which are then steeped in Cognac. It was believed to have been Napoleon Bonaparte's favourite tipple, hence the name.

Tangerine

The name tangerine is sometimes used to describe the mandarin family but it has no real meaning: the term is thought to have come from the United States where the seeds from an old variety called Moragne tangerine were cultivated by Colonel F.L. Dancy. The Dancy tangerine was the result and tangerine has now become the accepted American name for a mandarin. Another theory as to the origin of its name is that the fruit was called tangerine after the town of Tangier, when mandarins were imported from Morocco.

Below: These mandarins, grown in Italy, have sweet flesh, but often contain a large number of pips (seeds).

POMELO AND UGLI FRUIT

Large and ungainly looking, these fruit are worth keeping an eye out for as they have a refreshing, delicious flavour.

Pomelo or Shaddock, *Citrus grandis*

Originally from Malaysia and Indonesia, pomelo seeds were taken from that part of the world to Barbados by English explorers and settlers in the 17th century. The pomelo was first introduced by a sea captain called Shaddock, hence its alternative name.

This fruit is the largest member of the citrus family, often with 16 segments as opposed to the 12 in its descendant, the grapefruit. There are three types – Thai, Indonesian and Chinese, each with several sub-species. Pomelos are considerably larger than grapefruit, and have thick yellow dimpled skin, pinky-yellow to deep red flesh and a sharp, refreshing flavour, which is improved with a sprinkling of sugar. They are used mostly in Asian and Thai cooking.

Look out for a new hybrid, the result of crossing a pomelo with a grapefruit. It is often labelled pummelo and has a smooth skin. If you come across one, the best way to prepare it is to cut it into segments as with an orange.

Ugli fruit

This citrus fruit owes its parentage to the grapefruit, mandarin and Seville (Temple) orange. Discovered growing wild in Jamaica at the beginning of the 20th century, it was called Ugli simply because of its appearance, the name patented with the "i" instead of the "y". Slightly larger than a grapefruit, it has orange skin mottled with green, with a large core surrounded by sweet, juicy orange flesh. The large core makes it seem light for its size, so the normal rule of choosing citrus that seem heavy in the hand does not apply. To eat, cut it in half, loosen the segments and spoon them out.

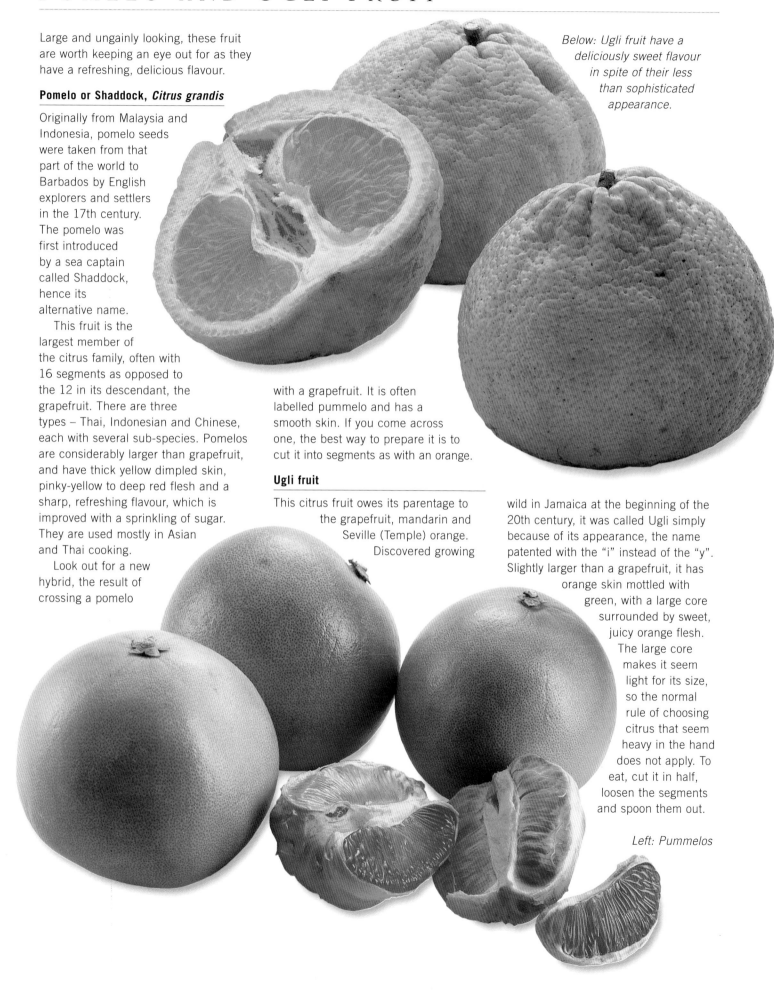

Below: Ugli fruit have a deliciously sweet flavour in spite of their less than sophisticated appearance.

Left: Pummelos

GRAPEFRUIT

It may not be so easy to peel as an orange or mandarin, but the grapefruit still has much to offer, and the ruby varieties are almost as sweet as their orange-fleshed cousins. All grapefruit have a refreshing, acidic flavour.

History

Both oranges and pomelos grew in Barbados in the 17th century, and it is thought that the grapefruit originated here, the result of a natural cross between the two.

The grapefruit was later introduced into Florida by Odette Phillipe, a French count, and production began in earnest at the end of the 19th century. Florida is still the major grower, followed by California, Mexico, Cuba, Argentina, South Africa, Israel and Cyprus. The name grapefruit is believed to reflect the way the fruit grows on the tree – in clusters, rather than as individual fruit – and has nothing to do with its flavour.

Varieties

There are two types: the white and the pigmented grapefruit, which is pink or ruby. White grapefruit, in fact, have bright yellow skins and flesh. There is also a sweet, emerald green variety, appropriately called Sweetie.

Right: The flesh of pink grapefruit can range from rosy pink to deep pink. As a general rule, the pinker the colour, the sweeter the grapefruit.

**White grapefruit, *Citrus paradisi*
Marsh** First grown as the Marsh Seedless by E. H. Tison in 1886, this grapefruit is now commonly known simply as the Marsh. Slightly smaller than the Duncan – about 11cm/4⅓in in diameter – it has a thicker rind. Nowadays, it is the most widely grown variety worldwide.

Duncan The first Duncan tree was grown in 1830 in Florida, and all other commercially cultivated varieties of grapefruit come from this one. It has firm, juicy flesh with a rich sweet flavour, and it is the most popular variety for canning.

Above: White Marsh grapefruit have pale yellow flesh.

Pigmented grapefruit These grapefruit get their colour from the pigment lycopene. They have varietal names such as Henderson and Ray Ruby, but are seldom labelled as such in the supermarket. You are more likely to find them marketed collectively under names such as Ruby Sweet and Sunrise. All pigmented grapefruits are sweet and juicy. In today's health-conscious world, they are proving more popular than their paler parents, as they need no extra sugar.

Nutrition

Grapefruit are a good source of vitamins A and C, with the usual citrus minerals of calcium, phosphorus and potassium. Pink grapefruit contains an astonishing five times the amount of vitamin A as white grapefruit. Although there's no way of establishing this when you buy the fruit, it is interesting to note that grapefruit that crop in autumn have the highest levels of vitamin C. The peel is a source of bioflavonoids and this, together with the vitamin C content, will help to keep gums strong, arteries healthy and the immune system functioning well.

Buying and storing

Look for plump, firm fruit. The first rule when buying any of the varieties of grapefruit is to choose specimens that weigh heavy in the hand. The skin can be thick or thin, depending on the variety, but if it is puffy, there won't be much juice. Avoid fruit with blemishes on the skin. Grapefruit will

Right: Duncan grapefruit grows up to 17cm/7in in diameter, and is the most popular variety for canning.

keep for about one week if stored in the refrigerator.

Serving ideas

The days when the height of sophistication meant sprinkling a cut grapefruit with brown sugar, grilling (broiling) it and then placing half a glacé (candied) cherry precisely in the middle are long gone but, minus the cherry, this is still a delicious way to serve this type of citrus, as is brushing with melted butter and grilling. At breakfast, the juice awakens the taste buds, while the fibre keeps the digestive system in good working order. The juice can also be used in a marinade, and it tastes great in a vinaigrette dressing.

As a first course, grapefruit goes particularly well with seafood – try a mixture of prawns (shrimp), avocado and grapefruit – and provides a flavour contrast to the richness of smoked fish. You can use segments from pink and red varieties in fruit salads and sorbets (sherbets). The candied peel can be coated in melted chocolate and left to set, then served as an after-dinner treat. The fruit also makes an excellent marmalade.

Commercial uses

Half the world crop is made into juice, with the rest being eaten fresh or canned.

Left: As its name suggests, Sweetie needs no sugar.

OTHER EXOTIC CITRUS FRUIT

Modern transportation and the curiosity of contemporary cooks means that even the lesser known types of citrus are becoming familiar. We may not find them all in our local store, but could certainly encounter them when we travel in their countries of origin.

Kumquat

It wasn't until Robert Fortune, an English plant expert, brought kumquat plants to the Royal Botanical Gardens, that the English got their first taste of this fascinating fruit, which must be grown under glass if it is to survive the British winter. Kumquats, which originated in central China, were originally classified as citrus, then later assigned to their own genus, Fortunella, named to commemorate Mr Fortune. They are not grown commercially in the UK, but are cultivated in Israel, Morocco, Florida, Brazil and Australia, with smaller crops in Corsica and in France.

There are three varieties of these miniature orange lookalikes – Oval, Round and Large Round. All are about the size of a large olive, and can be eaten whole. The soft peel is sweeter than the flesh but even so, they are an acquired taste eaten raw and are best bottled with sugar and alcohol or simmered in sugar syrup.

Kumquats can be sliced and used in sweet and savoury salads, and are often served with duck, red meat, cheese or ice cream. They go very well with bitter salad leaves such as

Below: Limequats

chicory (Belgian endive) and frisée, and are excellent chopped and mixed with the stuffing for turkey. They make great marmalade and jam, and taste delectable when dipped in chocolate. Their thick skin means that they travel and keep well. Store in the refrigerator for up to one week.

Kumquat hybrids

New citrus hybrids are constantly appearing, sometimes naturally, other times through experimentation.
Orangequat This is a cross between the sweet orange and kumquat, and can be eaten fresh or used in cooking.

Limequat A cross between the Mexican lime and the kumquat, the main varieties of limequats are Eustis and Lakeland. If you come across them while they are still green, you can use them in cooking in the same way as limes.

Sudachi

A true citrus fruit, the sudachi has a firm, thick, green skin, light yellow flesh and fairly large pips (seeds). The juice and finely grated rind are used in Japanese cooking, especially with fish and in combination with matsutake (pine mushrooms), but the fruit is rarely seen in other countries. It has a similar flavour to limes, which may be used in its place in cooking.

Below: Sudachi

Below: Kumquats can be eaten whole – skin and all – although you will need to discard the pips (seeds).

Citron, *Citrus medica*

This ancient ancestor of the lemon is believed to come from the foothills of the Himalayas, though it may also have come from China. Records show it was transported to the Middle East by the Medians in the 7th century BC. Media, from which the botanical name derives, is now part of Iran. This was where the Greeks came to know and value the citron. The Romans also appreciated the fruit, and used to soak the rind in fish sauce. After the Roman Empire fell, the citron became an important part of Arab cuisine.

Below: Candied green citron peel, with candied orange and grapefruit peel.

It is a large fruit, up to 30cm/12in long. It yields very little juice, but this is not important, as it is the aromatic thick, knobbly, greenish skin that is of most interest to the cook.

The citron is used in religious ceremonies, particularly in India, where Kuvera, the god of wealth, is depicted holding a citron; and a variety called etrog is essential in the celebration of the Jewish festival of Sukkot.

Citrons are cultivated in China, Japan, Greece, Corsica, Italy, Morocco and Israel, but only on a small scale. When it is grown commercially, the main reason is to utilize the peel, which, when candied, develops a lovely translucency. On the island of Corsica, citrons are used to make a liqueur called *Cédratine*, a rich, smooth drink usually drunk straight.

Left: Bergamot is used for confectionery and pâtisserie, as well as perfumery.

One weird and wonderful variety is the Buddha's Hand, or Fingered Citron, which has about a dozen orange-yellow, finger-like protuberances, This fruit is inedible, but the scented skin makes them popular as room fresheners. The Chinese like to hang them in wardrobes to perfume their clothes.

Bergamot, *Citrus bergamia*

Not to be confused with the herb of the same name, the bergamot orange looks a bit like a large lime. The sour-tasting fruit is not grown for its eating qualities – although the peel makes excellent marmalade – but for the essential oil in the extremely aromatic rind. This is used in perfumery and confectionery, and, most famously, as a flavouring for Earl Grey tea. Tobacco is sometimes perfumed with bergamot oil, as is the barley sugar made in the French town of Nancy.

Known in the Mediterranean for centuries, the bergamot orange is today cultivated commercially in Calabria in Italy, with smaller crops coming from Turkey and the Ivory Coast in West Africa.

Above: The etrog, a variety of citron, is used in the Jewish festival of Sukkot, a celebration of the harvest. The fruit is considered unfit if it is dried up, too small, spotted or if the protuberance at the tip has been broken off.

EQUIPMENT

Although you can squeeze an orange with your bare hands, the job is made much easier with equipment designed especially for the job, whether this be a simple reamer or a sophisticated juicer. There are several other inexpensive gadgets that will prove handy in the citrus kitchen.

Vegetable peeler

Use a vegetable peeler to pare away thin strips of citrus rind, leaving the white pith behind. There are two types to choose from – the fixed blade peeler, which demands little dexterity in the hands of the user, but doesn't cut quite such a fine strip, and the swivel-blade peeler, which is sharper and more flexible and therefore more precise.

Cannelle knife (zester)

This handy tool has a tooth-like blade, which will shave citrus rind into ribbons or into fine julienne strips, leaving all the bitter white pith behind.

Citrus zester

Scrape the five-hole blade of the citrus zester over oranges, lemons or limes and the peel will come off in fine curly ribbons. A useful combination tool, which is both a citrus zester and a cannelle knife, is also available.

Citrus reamer

This curvy wooden device is simple but effective, letting you squeeze the juice straight into a bowl or pan. You simply insert the pointed end into a halved lemon or other

Above: Cannelle knife (left) and combination citrus zester and cannelle knife (right)

Below: Citrus reamer

Left: Fixed- and swivel-blade vegetable peelers

citrus fruit, and twist. Its only drawback is that you can't catch the pips (seeds), but if you hold the halved fruit in one hand with slightly opened fingers, and carefully twist the reamer with the other, you should be able to catch them. Alternatively, squeeze the juice into a jug (pitcher), then strain it into the bowl or pan.

Below: Lemon squeezer

Lemon squeezer

Most of us have one of these tucked away in the kitchen. The basic design has barely changed in generations, but they now come in a variety of shapes, sizes and materials – glass, plastic or chrome. The business end of the utensil is a dome on to which you push a halved fruit, then twist to extract the juice. All the pips are trapped in the rim and the juice either flows into a simple channel surrounding the dome, or into

a bowl beneath. Some models have interchangeable heads, which allows them to be used for anything from a small lime to a large grapefruit.

Citrus press

If you want to squeeze the maximum amount of juice from the minimum quantity of fruit, this is well worth the investment. The simplest version is a hand-operated gadget with a geared lever mechanism. As you pull the lever forward, the juice is squeezed into the integral container. A wide range of electric juicers is also available.

Below: A hand-operated citrus press

Box grater

Choose a grater with as many different grating surfaces as possible, preferably with a handle for a better grip. Make sure it stands firmly on the work surface or in a bowl, if you prefer to grate directly into that. Some models include a flat blade for thinly slicing lemons and limes, too.

Microplane grater

A real revolution when it comes to grating. The blade is actually a chemically sharpened grating surface that will take the outer rind off a lemon in next to no time, and with very little effort. It comes with an extremely comfortable soft grip handle, and it is very easy to brush off every last bit of grated rind from the back when it comes to cleaning.

Grapefruit knife

This is a small knife with a slim, serrated blade, which is curved to follow the natural shape of

Left: Grapefruit knife with curved blade

Right: A microplane grater makes speedy work of grating citrus rind.

Left: Box grater

the halved fruit. It makes short work of segmenting any type of citrus fruit.

Preserving pan

If you want to make marmalade, you will need a preserving pan. They come with a thick, heavy base to prevent burning and a sturdy handle, so that you can get a good grip as you lift the pan off the stove. The best preserving pan will also be wide and fairly shallow, which makes for rapid, highly effective boiling. Choose a pan that is made from stainless steel or pristine (that is, not cracked) enamel: avoid aluminium, which will taint the fruit. Preserving pans also come with a non-stick lining.

Right: Sugar thermometer

Below: Preserving pan with a square of muslin (cheesecloth) for straining marmalades.

Tips for grating citrus rind

• Grate citrus fruit on to a sheet of foil or baking parchment. You can then tip it into a bowl or pan.
• Use a small pastry brush or even a new toothbrush to remove the grated rind from the grater.
• Make sure that you only grate the coloured rind and not the bitter-tasting white pith.

Sugar thermometer

Expert marmalade makers will know just when it is ready to be potted, but for most of us, a sugar thermometer is the best and most accurate way to check the temperature, and also to determine just when the setting point has been reached.

BASIC TECHNIQUES

Preparing citrus for use in cooking, to eat fresh or for decoration, is not hard but it does help to master a few techniques. The cheering colours of citrus make it an ideal fruit for use in decoration, and even simple touches enliven dishes.

The following techniques are shown with the fruit most likely to demand that particular skill, but they can be used sucessfully with most citrus fruit.

Peeling and segmenting oranges

1 Using a serrated knife, cut a small slice off both the top and bottom of the orange or other fruit to expose the flesh and make it easier to remove the peel.

2 Holding the orange in one hand, cut off the peel in one continuous strip, starting at the top and cutting around the orange in a circular motion, using a gentle sawing action and making sure that you remove every scrap of white pith. Alternatively, stand the orange on a plate and cut off the peel in strips, working from top to bottom.

3 Holding the fruit over a bowl to catch all the juices, remove each segment in turn by cutting down either side of the membrane and easing it away.

4 When you have removed all the segments, squeeze the membrane over the bowl to extract the remaining juice.

Zesting and grating a lemon

If you intend to use the rind or peel of any fruit in cooking, choose an unwaxed or organic fruit or scrub thoroughly waxed fruit first.

1 To zest a lemon, hold the fruit very firmly in one hand. Scrape a lemon zester down the length of the fruit.

2 If you need the zest to be even finer, brush it into a neat pile on a chopping board, hold a large chef's knife at right angles to the board and rock it back and forth.

3 To grate a lemon, hold it against the fine side of the grater and work it up and down, taking off only the zest and not the pith. Work over a small bowl or a piece of foil to catch the rind.

Paring and cutting julienne strips

Julienne is the term used for fine strips or sticks. Choose fruit with firm, but not too thick rind, such as lemon and lime.

1 Wash and dry the fruit, then, using a swivel-blade vegetable peeler, remove long, wide strips of rind. Do not include the bitter white pith.

2 Square off the ends of the strips, then cut them lengthways. Use immediately or set aside, covered with cold water.

Segmenting grapefruit

Fresh grapefruit is delicious first thing in the morning. Serve it in its shell, with the segments loosened for easy eating.

1 Cut the fruit in half and remove the pips (seeds). Use a grapefruit knife with a curved blade to cut around between the skin and the flesh.

2 Loosen the segments by cutting between the membrane that surrounds each segment. Start in the centre, work out towards the skin, then cut around and back to the middle again.

3 Lastly, cut out the central core of the fruit and remove as much of the white membrane as you can before serving.

Drying mandarin rind

When dried, the peel of mandarins and other similar thin-skinned citrus fruit gives a wonderful flavour to meat stews and casseroles, and it can also be used in soups, vegetable dishes, sauces, salad dressings, desserts and cakes.

1 Wash unwaxed fruit thoroughly, then peel. Cut the peel into large pieces and place each piece on a board, skin-side down. Use a small knife to scrape away every trace of white pith.

2 Cut the peel into thin strips, about 2.5cm/1in long, and spread these out on a tray. Cover loosely and leave to dry in an airy room for about one week, until they are completely dry and have darkened in colour. Alternatively, dry in an oven preheated to 110°C/225°F/ Gas ¼ for 10–12 hours, then leave until completely cold.

3 Tip the peel into a clean, screwtop jar, replace the lid and keep in a cool, dry place. Use the rind whole, crumble between your fingers or powder in a coffee grinder. One or two strips, or 5ml/1 tsp ground peel, will be enough to flavour most dishes.

Making a citrus bouquet garni

In Provence in the South of France, it is traditional to add a strip of citrus rind to the herbs in a bouquet garni, especially when it is to be used to flavour a beef stew or casserole. It would also go well in rich game and duck dishes.

1 Pare a broad strip of rind from an orange or mandarin. A clementine or satsuma could be used instead, but avoid very thin-skinned fruit. Remove any white pith from the rind.

2 Tie the rind in a neat bundle with a sprig each of fresh thyme and rosemary and a few stalks of fresh parsley. Add a bay leaf if you like. Leave the end of the string long enough to loop around the handle of a pan or casserole. This prevents them from dispersing through the stew or casserole and also makes for easy retrieval before serving.

VARIATION

If a bouquet garni is to be used in fish or shellfish recipes, use lemon or grapefruit rind instead of orange or mandarin, and add a sprig of fresh tarragon and dill. If you like, tie the bouquet with a thin strip of celery.

Making caramelized citrus rind

The bold yellows and greens of lemons and limes combine to make a pretty decoration on cakes and desserts, such as Key lime pie or lemon and lime cheesecake. The caramelized rind is sweet, with an underlying citrus tang.

1 Using a swivel-bladed vegetable peeler, remove the rind from washed, unwaxed lemons and limes in long, even strips. Using a small, sharp knife, slice into fine julienne strips.

2 Place the strips in a small pan of water, bring to the boil, then lower the heat and simmer for about 5 minutes. Drain, refresh under cold water and then drain again. Pat dry with kitchen paper. Line a grill (broiler) pan with foil and preheat the grill.

3 Spread out the rind flat on a sheet of baking parchment and dredge with icing (confectioners') sugar. Toss to coat, then tip on to the foil-lined grill pan. Grill (broil) for 2–3 minutes, or until the sugar just begins to melt, then leave to cool and harden. Pile on top of a cooled cake or dessert, dusting with more icing sugar, if you like.

Making citrus corkscrews

Hang these over the edge of ice cream dishes or use to decorate a cocktail flavoured with citrus juice.

1 Using a cannelle knife (zester), pare long strips of rind from a lemon, lime or orange. The strips should be as long as it is possible to make them.

2 Pick up a cocktail stick (toothpick) and wind and twist the strip of citrus rind tightly around it. Slide the cocktail stick out, and you will be left with a little citrus corkscrew. Make more in the same way.

Making citrus loops

1 Cut a lemon in half lengthways, then cut each half into four equal segments. Holding one segment in your hand, use a sharp knife to ease away the flesh from the skin in a single piece, leaving about 1cm/½in still attached at the top.

2 Carefully cut away any bitter, white pith still remaining on the now bare piece of lemon peel, then fold it under the flesh segment to form a loop. Make three more lemon loops from the remaining segments.

Making citrus curls

These have a delicacy and elegance that makes them the ideal decoration for a citrus mousse.

1 Using a cannelle knife (zester), carefully pare the rind, avoiding the white pith.

2 Dust the curls with caster (superfine) sugar until coated.

Making citrus leaves

Two of these, placed side by side, make a dramatic garnish for a salmon terrine.

Cut a V-shaped wedge from the side of the lemon. Cut the lemon lengthways in slices, following the curve created by removing the wedge.

Making citrus shells

Oranges, lemons and limes look lovely filled with ice cream, sorbet (sherbet) or mousse. Grapefruit shells are a little large for desserts, but are wonderful for individual salads, such as grapefruit, prawn (shrimp) and watercress.

1 Cut the top off the fruit and set it aside to use as a lid. Loosen the flesh by running the blade of a small, sharp knife between the flesh and the skin. Scoop out the flesh with a teaspoon, keeping the shell intact, and set it aside for another dessert. Rinse the shell and leave it upside down to drain. Make more shells in the same way.

2 Pipe or spoon the filling into the fruit shells and replace the lids, setting them at an angle if you like. If the filling is ice cream or sorbet, wrap the filled fruit in clear film (plastic wrap) and freeze. If the filling is a mousse, cover loosely, chill and serve within the hour.

COOK'S TIP

To make shells more decorative, use a cannelle knife (zester) to make lengthways grooves in the skin of the fruit before cutting off the top and hollowing out the fruit.

Making a citrus ice bowl

This looks glorious filled with little balls of citrus sorbet (sherbet) or ice cream. Paler colours look more effective than bold ones.

1 You will need two freezerproof glass or plastic bowls that will fit one inside the other, leaving a gap between them of about 2.5cm/1in all around. Add some crushed ice to the larger bowl to hold up the inner bowl, then tape them together with parcel tape. It is essential to make sure that the gap between them is the same all the way around.

2 Put the pair of bowls on to a large plate to catch any drips. Carefully fill the gap between the bowls with water. It should come almost to the top, and the smaller bowl should float slightly.

3 Slide thin slices of lime, orange and lemon, with, perhaps, a few sliced kumquats, into the water between the bowls. Use a skewer to push them into position. Check the bowl from all angles until you have achieved an attractive and well-balanced effect. Carefully lift the bowls into the freezer and freeze overnight, until required.

4 To unmould the ice bowl, peel off the tape. Put the bowls in another larger bowl half-filled with hot water, then pour a little hot water into the smaller bowl. Leave it there for about 30 seconds or so, then lift both bowls out of the water. Pour the water out of the smaller bowl and loosen the inner bowl with a thin, round-bladed knife.

5 Lift out the inner bowl, turn out the ice bowl and put it on a large plate. You can sprinkle a few extra slices of citrus fruit or curled rind around the edge if you like, or add a few flowers, such as nasturtiums or calendula marigolds. Fill with scoops of ice cream or sorbet and serve.

COOK'S TIPS

• For a crystal-clear ice bowl, use water that has been boiled and then left to cool completely or use still mineral water; for a more frosted appearance, use water straight from the tap (faucet).
• If your ice bowl is to be part of a buffet, make the ice bowl in advance, unmould it, fill with ice cream or sorbet (sherbet), then put back into the freezer until required. Leave any final decorations to the last minute.

PRESERVING CITRUS

The tradition of preserving citrus goes back to the time when the fruit was a rare luxury. Today we are lucky to have a plentiful supply of fruit all year round, but it is still worth making preserves, if only to experience the wonderful depth of flavour that develops when orange peel is candied, kumquats are bottled in brandy syrup or Seville (Temple) oranges metamorphose into marmalade. The best time for preserving citrus is during the winter months when the fruit is at its juiciest.

Quick candied lemon slices

Translucent candied lemon slices look gorgeous on a fresh lemon tart. Use this method when you are going to serve the slices soon after candying.

1 Cut two large, thin-skinned, unwaxed lemons into thin slices, put them in a pan and cover with plenty of water. Simmer for 15–20 minutes, or until the skin is tender, then drain.

2 Put 200g/7oz/scant 1 cup caster (superfine) sugar in a large, shallow pan and stir in about 105ml/7 tbsp water. Heat until the sugar has all dissolved, stirring constantly, then bring to the boil. Boil for 2 minutes, add the lemon slices and cook for 10–15 minutes, until they look shiny and candied.

3 Lift the candied lemon slices out of the syrup using tongs or a slotted spoon and arrange them on top of a tart or cake. Return the syrup to the heat and boil, without stirring, until reduced to a thick glaze. Brush this over the lemon slices and leave to cool completely before serving.

Candying orange peel

When you squeeze oranges for juice, the peel is wasted. Transforming it into candied peel will provide you with a flavoursome ingredient for adding to fruit cakes, scones and desserts. When the candied peel is cool, store it in a clean jar and it will keep for months.

1 Choose unwaxed oranges with thick skins. Wash and dry them. Remove the rind in long thin strips. Using a sharp knife, cut the peel into julienne strips.

2 For each orange you use, put 250ml/8fl oz/1 cup water and 115g/4oz/½ cup granulated sugar into a pan. Stir well over a medium heat until the sugar has dissolved. Bring to the boil, add the strips of orange rind, half-cover the pan and simmer until the syrup has reduced by three-quarters. Remove the pan from the heat and leave to cool completely.

3 Preheat the oven to 110°C/225°F/Gas ¼. Sift icing (confectioners') sugar in a thick, even layer over a baking tray. Drop in the candied peel and roll the pieces in the sugar. Dry in the oven for 1–2 hours, checking often. When the strips are crisp, they are done.

Preserved lemons

These are surprisingly mild and sweet, despite the salt used to preserve them. Although they will be ready after a month, they'll keep for at least another six. They are used all over the Middle East and in North Africa, particularly Morocco, where they form an essential part of the flavouring for a traditional *tagine*. Add strips of preserved lemon to any lamb or chicken stew and you'll notice the difference. The following makes about 1.3kg/3lb.

1 Put 14 unwaxed lemons of average size in a large bowl and pour over cold water to cover. Cut 12 of the lemons into quarters, but keep them attached at one end.

2 Ease slightly apart the sections on one of the lemons, then spoon 5ml/1 tsp of sea salt into the centre. Close the lemon again. Repeat with the remaining fruit.

3 Pack the salted lemons in sterilized jars, sprinkling with salt, and pressing them down. Squeeze the juice of the remaining 2 lemons over the top, then top up with olive oil. Cover and seal, then store in a cool dark place.

Glacé citrus slices

These luxury sweetmeats are very popular, and if you make them yourself, they will cost just a fraction of the price in the stores.

MAKES 24–32 SLICES

INGREDIENTS
   450g/1lb citrus fruit, such as oranges, lemons, limes and clementines, along with apricots or cherries, according to the season
   1kg/2¼lb/4½ cups granulated sugar
   115g/4oz/1 cup powdered glucose

1 Wash and dry the fruit. Thinly slice the citrus fruit, remove the pits from apricots and prick the skins of cherries. Place enough in a preserving pan to cover the base, then cover with water. Simmer gently to avoid breaking the fruit. Using a slotted spoon, transfer to a shallow heatproof dish. Cook any remaining fruit in the same way.

2 Measure the liquid from the pan. You will need 300ml/½ pint/1¼ cups, so make it up with water if necessary. Tip it into the preserving pan and stir in 60ml/4 tbsp of the sugar. Add all the glucose. Heat gently until the sugar has dissolved. Bring to the boil and pour over the fruit in the dish, making sure they are submerged. Leave overnight.

3 Next day, drain the syrup into the pan and add a further 60ml/4 tbsp sugar. Dissolve the sugar and bring to the boil. Pour over the fruit and leave overnight. Repeat this process on the next five days, so that the syrup becomes more and more concentrated.

4 On the next day – day 8 – repeat the process of draining the concentrated syrup into the pan, but this time add 90ml/6 tbsp sugar. Bring to the boil, stirring, then add the fruit to the pan and cook them gently for about 3 minutes. Return the fruit and syrup to the dish and leave for two days.

5 On day 10, repeat the process carried out on day 8. The syrup will now look like honey. Having returned the fruit to the dish, leave it for at least ten days, or up to three weeks.

6 Preheat the oven to 110°C/225°F/ Gas ¼. Place a wire rack over a baking tray. Using a fork or tongs, transfer the fruit to the rack in a single layer. Dry in the oven for 1–2 hours, until they no longer feel sticky.

7 To coat the slices in sugar, briefly dip each slice in boiling water, then roll in granulated sugar. To coat in syrup, place the remaining sugar in a pan, add 175ml/6fl oz/¾ cup water and heat gently until dissolved. Boil for 1 minute. Dip each citrus slice into boiling water, then into the syrup. Place on the wire rack and leave in a warm place to dry.

Spiced poached kumquats

These are ideal served after Christmas or Thanksgiving, with the rich pickings left over from the previous day's feast. Cold turkey, ham – even sausages – will all be enhanced by this preserve.

MAKES ABOUT 900G/2LB

INGREDIENTS
   500g/1¼lb kumquats
   350ml/12fl oz/1½ cups white wine vinegar
   500g/1¼lb/2½ cups granulated sugar
   1 cinnamon stick
   15 cloves
   6 allspice berries

1 Cut the kumquats in quarters and remove the pips (seeds). Place the kumquats in a large heavy pan and pour in just enough water to cover. Bring to the boil, then lower the heat and simmer until the fruit is tender.

2 With a slotted spoon, remove the kumquats from the pan and set them aside. Add the vinegar, sugar, cinnamon stick, cloves and allspice berries to the cooking liquid and bring to the boil, stirring only occasionally. Return the kumquats to the pan, lower the heat and simmer for 30 minutes.

3 Carefully lift the kumquats out of the syrup and place them in jars that have been sterilized with boiling water and warmed in the oven. Boil the syrup until thick and syrupy. Pour the syrup over the kumquats, cover and leave in a cool place for at least two weeks before using.

MARMALADES

Breakfast just wouldn't be the same without marmalade. The name comes from the Portuguese *marmelada*, which was a sweet, stiff paste made from quinces. In Tudor times, peach, apple, pear, lemon and orange pastes were all called marmalades. Resembling fruit cheeses, they were usually cut into pieces and presented in fancy boxes as a sweetmeat. By the 18th century, a clear, looser version existed, which was a precursor to today's preserves. Then and now, Seville (Temple) oranges, grapefruit, lemons and limes are the most popular fruits to use.

Seville orange marmalade

This classic recipe is made with the best oranges for the job: Sevilles.

MAKES ABOUT 4KG/9½LB

INGREDIENTS
    1kg/2¼lb Seville oranges
    1 unwaxed lemon
    2.2 litres/4 pints/9 cups water
    2kg/4½lb/9 cups preserving sugar

1 Wash the oranges and lemon and cut them into quarters. Remove the flesh, pips (seeds) and pulp and tie them in a square of muslin (cheesecloth). Shred the peel finely or coarsely, depending on how you like your marmalade.

2 Place the peel in a preserving pan and add the water and the muslin bag. Bring to the boil, then lower the heat and simmer for 1½–2 hours. About 15 minutes before the peel is ready, preheat the oven to 110°C/225°F/ Gas ¼. Put the sugar in a heatproof bowl and place it in the oven to warm.

3 Remove the muslin bag and hold it over the pan between two plates. Press to extract as much liquid as possible. Stir in the sugar until it has dissolved, then boil rapidly until setting point is reached. Pour into warm, sterilized jars and seal. Label when cold.

Clementine and coriander marmalade

This marmalade has a sweet and spicy flavour that goes well with toast, but also with cold meats or hot sausages.

MAKES ABOUT 2.75KG/6LB

INGREDIENTS
    1.6kg/3½lb clementines, washed
    6 unwaxed lemons, washed
    30ml/2 tbsp coriander seeds, roasted
      and coarsely crushed
    3 litres/5 pints/12 cups water
    1.6kg/3½lb preserving sugar

1 Cut the fruit in half, then squeeze and pour the juice into a preserving pan.

2 Scrape the pith from the citrus shells and tie it up, with the pips (seeds) and half the coriander, in a square of muslin (cheesecloth). Tie the bag to the handle of the pan so it dangles in the juice.

3 Slice the peel into shreds and add them to the pan with the water. Bring to the boil, then simmer for 1½ hours. Preheat the oven to 110°C/225°F/ Gas ¼. Put the sugar in a heatproof bowl and place it in the oven to warm.

4 Remove the muslin bag. Hold it over the pan and squeeze it between two plates to extract all the liquid. Stir in the sugar and the remaining coriander, then boil rapidly until setting point is reached. Skim off any scum, then leave for about 30 minutes. Pour into sterilized jars and cover with waxed discs. Leave to cool before sealing and labelling the jars.

Tips for a successful marmalade
The best way to test for setting point is with a sugar thermometer. When it registers about 105°C/ 220°F, the marmalade is ready.

To sterilize jars, preheat the oven to the highest setting. Wash the jars in hot, soapy water, then rinse. Stand them in the sink and pour over boiling water. Place them on a baking tray in the oven for 10 minutes.

Three fruit marmalade

You could use sweet oranges, such as Valencia or Navelina, in place of the bitter Seville oranges, but the flavour of the marmalade would not be so intense and tangy. Most marmalades require all the pith to be included on the peel, but in this case, err on the cautious side and don't have it too thick.

MAKES ABOUT 2.25KG/5LB

INGREDIENTS
   2 unwaxed or well-scrubbed
      Seville oranges
   2 unwaxed lemons
   1 grapefruit
   1.75 litres/3 pints/7½ cups water
   1.5kg/3lb/6¾ cups
      preserving sugar

1 Wash the fruit and cut them in half. Squeeze all the fruit and pour the juice into a preserving pan. Tie the pips (seeds) and pulp securely in a square of muslin (cheesecloth). Tie the bag to the handle of the pan so that it dangles in the citrus juice.

Marmalade or jam?
The main difference between marmalade and jam is that the former invariably contains citrus fruit. Oranges, lemons and limes are used to make fruit curds or cheeses, but we seldom find them in jam, except in order to boost pectin levels. One exception, however, is a light orange jam, from Portugal, which makes a delicious spread.

2 Cut the citrus skins into thin wedges; scrape off and discard the membranes and pith. Cut the peel in slivers and add them to the pan with the water. Bring to simmering point and cook gently for 2 hours, or until all the peel is tender and the water has reduced by half.

3 About 15 minutes before the peel is ready, preheat the oven to 110°C/225°F/ Gas ¼. Put the sugar in a heatproof bowl and place in the oven to warm.

4 Remove the muslin bag. Holding it over the pan, squeeze it between two plates to extract all the liquid. Stir in the sugar until dissolved.

5 Bring to the boil and boil rapidly until setting point is reached. Pour a small amount on to a chilled saucer. Chill for 2 minutes, then push the marmalade with your finger; if wrinkles form on the surface, it is ready.

6 Skim off any scum from the surface, then leave the marmalade to stand for 30 minutes. Stir, then pour into warm, sterilized jars and cover with waxed discs. Leave to cool before adding the lids and labelling the jars.

Other citrus marmalades
Toast was invented for delicious treats like these.

Lime marmalade Wash 450g/1lb limes, then slice them thinly, removing the pips (seeds) and putting them in a small muslin (cheesecloth) bag. Put the lime slices and bag of pips in a large pan and pour in 1.5 litres/ 2½ pints/6 cups water. Leave overnight to soften the lime rind, which can be tough. Next day, bring the water to the boil, simmer for 1¼–1½ hours until the lime rind is tender. Remove the muslin bag, squeeze out all the liquid between two plates and stir 1.2kg/2½lb/5 cups preserving sugar into the pan. Continue as for Three Fruit Marmalade.

Kumquat marmalade Halve 1.3kg/ 3lb kumquats and scoop out the pips (seeds). Peel and segment one orange and one lemon, then chop the segments coarsely, removing any tough membrane and pips. Put the citrus flesh in a pan with the kumquat halves and tie everything else in a muslin (cheesecloth) bag. Add 750ml/ 1¼ pints/3 cups water. Bring to the boil, then simmer for about 30 minutes, until the kumquats are tender. Remove the muslin bag and squeeze out all the liquid between two plates. Carefully stir 675g/1½lb/3 cups preserving sugar into the pan. Continue as for Three Fruit Marmalade.

CITRUS CURDS

Strictly speaking, citrus curds are not preserves as they contain butter and eggs, but they still make great spreads.

Lemon curd

Creamy, buttery and tangy, lemon curd is well worth making yourself. The home-made version tastes nothing like the bright yellow bought stuff, which owes its set more to copious amounts of cornflour (cornstarch) than eggs. Use lemon curd to fill a sponge cake, flavour a trifle or stir it through vanilla ice cream for a quick sweet sensation. Best of all, spoon it generously on to a thick slice of fresh white bread, spread with a little unsalted (sweet) butter.

MAKES ABOUT 450G/1LB

INGREDIENTS
    3 unwaxed lemons
    115g/4oz/½ cup caster
      (superfine) sugar
    15ml/1 tbsp cornflour (cornstarch),
      mixed to a paste with
      15ml/1 tbsp water
    2 egg yolks
    50g/2oz/¼ cup unsalted
      (sweet) butter

1 Grate the lemons and squeeze the juice. Add to a pan with the sugar and stir over a low heat to dissolve the sugar. Stir in the cornflour paste.

2 Remove from the heat and whisk in the egg yolks. Return to a low heat, whisk for about 2 minutes; remove from the heat. Gradually whisk in the butter. Pour into a sterilized jar, cover and seal at once. Leave to cool, then store in the refrigerator and use within three weeks.

Lemon and lime curd

The tart lime rind and juice gives this spread an added dimension. It makes a lovely filling for a roulade.

MAKES ABOUT 800G/1¾LB

INGREDIENTS
    3 large unwaxed lemons
    3 unwaxed limes
    175g/6oz/¾ lb unsalted
      (sweet) butter
    225g/8oz/1 cup caster
      (superfine) sugar
    4 large (US extra large) eggs, beaten

1 Wash the lemons and limes and finely grate the rinds.

2 Squeeze the juice from the lemons and limes, then strain it into a bowl.

3 Melt the butter in a heatproof bowl set over a pan of barely simmering water or in the top of a double boiler. Beat in the citrus rind and juice, the sugar and eggs. Cook, beating constantly, until the mixture is smooth and thickened. Do not let it boil. Pour the curd into warm, sterilized jars and seal. When cold, store in the refrigerator for three weeks.

Passion fruit and lemon curd

This tastes wonderful when stirred into thick yogurt or spooned over ice cream.

MAKES ABOUT 450G/1LB

INGREDIENTS
    2 passion fruit
    1 lemon
    175g/6oz/¾ cup unsalted
      (sweet) butter
    115g/4oz/½ cup caster
      (superfine) sugar
    2 egg yolks

1 Cut the passion fruit in half and strain all the pulp and seeds into a bowl. Cut the lemon in half and squeeze the juice. Strain it into the bowl.

2 Melt the butter in the top of a double boiler or in a heatproof bowl set over a pan of barely simmering water. Beat in the passion fruit pulp, lemon juice, sugar and egg yolks. Cook, beating constantly, until the mixture thickens. Do not let it boil. Pour into a warm sterilized jar and seal. When cold, store in the refrigerator for three weeks.

> **Tips for successful citrus curds**
> • The important thing to remember when making citrus curd is to stir it constantly and avoid letting it boil. If you are not confident about making it in a heavy pan, use a double boiler.
> • Stabilize the mixture by adding 10ml/2 tsp cornflour (cornstarch) mixed to a paste with some water. Add to the mixture before the eggs.

CITRUS IN ALCOHOL

Fruit can be preserved very successfully in alcohol, as 18th-century sailors discovered when they macerated their booty of tropical fruits in rum. The liquor takes on the flavour of the fruit, while the fruit absorbs the alcohol.

Orange brandy

This traditional English recipe produces a delicious drink with a flavour similar to that of orange liqueur. It is ready to drink within about three weeks of being bottled, but tastes even better if left for longer. The following makes about 750ml/1¼ pints/3 cups.

1 Thinly pare the rind from one lemon and two oranges, taking care to remove only the bright outer layer. Cut the rind in julienne strips and put it in a large earthenware bowl.

2 Add 225g/8oz/1 cup preserving sugar and a pinch of saffron, then pour in a 70cl bottle of brandy. Stir well.

3 Cover and set aside for three days. Stir four times a day. Strain, bottle and seal. Store in a cool, dark place for at least three weeks before opening.

Alternative spirits

Brandy and rum are popular and the most commonly used spirits for preserving citrus fruits, but liqueurs can also be used. Orange or mandarin liqueurs, such as Cointreau, Grand Marnier, Van der Hum and Mandarine Napoléon are obvious choices, but Kirsch and cherry brandy also work well.

Satsumas in brandy

Serve these juicy satsumas straight from the jar or gently heated. They make a delicious dessert accompanied by ice cream or cream, with a little of the brandy poured over. The satsumas are preserved in brandy here, but you could happily substitute it with an orange- or mandarin-flavoured liqueur. The following makes about 1.3kg/3lb.

1 Peel the satsumas, making sure you remove every last trace of the bitter, white pith.

2 Weigh them, place them in a large bowl and cover with the same weight of caster sugar. Cover the bowl and leave for 1 hour. Approximately 1kg/2¼lb each of peeled fruit and sugar will need a 70cl bottle of brandy.

3 Spoon the sugared fruit into cold, sterilized preserving jars and then pour in just enough brandy to cover the satsumas.

4 Seal the jars and store in a cool, dark place. Leave for at least two months before using, although the fruit will keep for up to six months.

Kumquats in Cointreau

These bright orange kumquats look truly spectacular and taste very good, too. Serve spooned over ice cream or mixed into fresh fruit salads.

MAKES ABOUT 675G/1½LB

INGREDIENTS
  450g/1lb kumquats, or a mixture of kumquats and limequats
  175g/6oz/¾ cup granulated sugar
  300ml/½ pint/1¼ cups water
  150ml/¼ pint/⅔ cup Cointreau
  15ml/1 tbsp orange flower water

1 Using a cocktail stick (toothpick), prick each fruit in several places.

2 Put the sugar in a heavy pan and pour in the water. Heat gently, stirring occasionally, until the sugar has dissolved. Bring to the boil.

3 Add the citrus fruit, lower the heat and simmer gently for 25 minutes, until it is tender, but still intact.

4 Using a slotted spoon, transfer the fruit to warm sterilized jars.

5 Boil the syrup until it reaches 107°C/225°F. If you do not have a sugar thermometer, test by pressing a small amount between two teaspoons. When they are pulled apart, a thread should form. Pour the syrup into a jug (pitcher).

6 Let the syrup cool slightly, then stir in the Cointreau and orange flower water. Pour over the fruit in the jars until covered. Seal immediately. Store in a cool place and use within six months.

CHUTNEYS AND RELISHES

There's something very satisfying about making your own chutneys, and the sight of jars with hand-written labels is always impressive. This type of preserve is easier to make than a marmalade, as you don't have to worry about setting points or skimming. Fresh chutneys and relishes are even easier.

Spicy chutney

Grated orange rind gives this dried fruit chutney real piquancy. Although it is intended as festive fare, it keeps well, and you'll still be enjoying it when summer comes around.

MAKES ABOUT 1.6KG/3½LB

INGREDIENTS
   grated rind of 1 orange
   450g/1lb cooking apples
   500g/1¼lb/3 cups luxury mixed
     dried fruit
   30ml/2 tbsp mixed (apple pie) spice
   150ml/¼ pint/⅔ cup cider vinegar
   350g/12oz/2 cups soft light
     brown sugar

1 Put the grated orange rind in a large, heavy pan. Cut the apples into quarters, remove the cores and skin, then chop coarsely. Add to the pan, with the dried fruit, mixed spice, vinegar and brown sugar. Heat gently, stirring constantly until all the sugar has dissolved.

2 Bring to the boil, then lower the heat and simmer for about 45 minutes, stirring frequently, until the mixture is thick. Stir more frequently towards the end of cooking, as it thickens. Ladle into warm sterilized jars, cover and seal. Keep for one month before using.

Fresh lemon and coriander chutney

This is a fresh chutney. It is not cooked, and it is made a few hours before being served, so that the flavours can blend.

MAKES ABOUT 475ML/16FL OZ/2 CUPS

INGREDIENTS
   115g/4oz/4 cups fresh coriander
     (cilantro) leaves
   1 fresh green chilli
   2 garlic cloves, coarsely chopped
   5ml/1 tsp salt
   2.5ml/½ tsp granulated sugar
   25ml/1½ tbsp lemon juice
   45ml/3 tbsp ground peanuts
   120ml/4fl oz/½ cup water

1 Put the coriander leaves on a board. Pile them in rough heaps, then chop them coarsely.

2 Cut the chilli in half lengthways. Scrape out the seeds and core, then chop the flesh coarsely.

3 Put all the ingredients in a blender or food processor and process together until smooth. Spoon the chutney into a bowl or jar, then cover and chill for 2–3 hours before serving.

Spiced cranberry and orange relish

This relish is a great one to serve with roast turkey, goose or duck. Eat within one week of making.

MAKES ABOUT 450G/1LB

INGREDIENTS
   225g/8oz cranberries, chopped
   1 onion, finely chopped
   150ml/¼ pint/⅔ cup port
   115g/4oz/½ cup caster
     (superfine) sugar
   finely grated rind and juice of
     1 orange
   2.5ml/½ tsp English (hot)
     mustard powder
   1.5ml/¼ tsp ground ginger
   1.5ml/¼ tsp ground cinnamon
   5ml/1 tsp cornflour (cornstarch)
   50g/2oz/⅓ cup raisins

1 Put the cranberries in a pan. Add the onion, port and sugar. Cook gently for about 10 minutes, stirring frequently, until the cranberries are tender.

2 Mix together the orange juice, mustard powder, ginger, cinnamon and cornflour in a bowl. Add the mixture to the pan.

3 Add the raisins and orange rind. Cook over a high heat, stirring constantly, until the mixture thickens, then lower the heat and simmer for 2 minutes. Cool, then spoon into a bowl or jar, cover and chill until ready to serve.

COOK'S TIP
When making chutneys and relishes, use a heavy pan that is large enough to leave room to stir the mixture well to prevent it from catching on the base.

Red onion, garlic and lemon relish

A powerful combination of sweet red onions, spices, hot chillies and citrus. Serve with kebabs or grilled fish.

MAKES ABOUT 450G/1LB

INGREDIENTS
    45ml/3 tbsp olive oil
    3 large red onions, sliced
    2 heads of garlic, separated into
      cloves and peeled
    10ml/2 tsp coriander seeds, crushed
    10ml/2 tsp light muscovado (brown)
      sugar, plus a little extra
    pinch of saffron threads
    45ml/3 tbsp warm water
    5cm/2in piece cinnamon stick
    2–3 whole dried red chillies
    2 fresh bay leaves
    30–45ml/2–3 tbsp sherry vinegar
    juice of ½ small orange
    30ml/2 tbsp chopped fresh or
      preserved lemon
    salt and ground black pepper

1 Heat the oil in a heavy pan. Stir in the onions, cover and cook over a very low heat for 10–15 minutes, stirring occasionally, until soft.

2 Add the garlic cloves and coriander seeds. Cover and cook for 5–8 minutes, until the garlic is soft.

3 Add a pinch of salt, plenty of pepper and the sugar. Cook, uncovered, for 5 minutes. Soak the saffron threads in the warm water for 5 minutes, then add to the onions, with the soaking water. Add the cinnamon stick, dried chillies and bay leaves. Stir in 30ml/2 tbsp of the sherry vinegar and the orange juice.

4 Cook over a low heat, uncovered, until the onions are soft. Stir in the lemon and cook for 5 minutes more. Taste and adjust the salt, sugar and/or vinegar, if necessary. The relish is best if left to stand for 24 hours.

Tropical lime relish

This colourful Indonesian side dish is served with almost every meal, but goes especially well with fish.

MAKES ABOUT 450G/1LB

INGREDIENTS
    1cm/½in cube shrimp paste
    1 small or ½ large fresh pineapple
    ½ cucumber, halved lengthways
    50g/2oz dried shrimp
    1 large fresh chilli, seeded and
      coarsely chopped
    juice of 1 large lime or lemon
    light brown sugar, to taste (optional)

1 To prepare the shrimp paste, wrap the cube in foil and dry-fry over a low heat for 5 minutes, turning occasionally.

2 Cut off both ends of the pineapple. Stand it upright, then slice off the skin from top to bottom.

3 Cut the pineapple flesh into slices and remove any remaining eyes. Chop each slice into small chunks and set aside.

4 Trim the cucumber and slice it thinly. Spread out the slices in a colander, sprinkle with salt and set aside.

5 Place the dried shrimp in a food processor and chop finely, then add the chilli. Unwrap the shrimp paste and add to the food processor, pour in the lime or lemon juice and process to a paste.

6 Rinse the cucumber, drain and dry on kitchen paper. Mix with the pineapple and chill. Just before serving, spoon in the spice mixture with sugar to taste, if you like. Mix well.

SALSAS AND DIPS

Great for all sorts of meals, salsas and dips are always a delight, and they do double duty as side dishes and sauces.

Fiery citrus salsa

This versatile salsa can be served with kebabs or sausages.

MAKES ABOUT 475ML/16FL OZ/2 CUPS

INGREDIENTS
 1 orange
 1 eating apple, peeled
 2 fresh red chillies, seeded
 1 garlic clove
 8 fresh mint leaves
 juice of 1 lemon
 salt and ground black pepper

1 Slice the ends off the orange so that it will stand upright. Slice off the peel. Holding the orange over a bowl, cut it into segments. Squeeze what remains of the orange over the bowl. Slice the apple into wedges and remove the core.

2 Put the chillies in a food processor or blender with the orange segments and juice, apple, garlic and mint. Process until smooth, then pour in the lemon juice. Season and serve.

Salsa verde

Serve this classic sauce over mashed potatoes or drizzled over grilled fish.

MAKES ABOUT 300ML/½ PINT/1¼ CUPS

INGREDIENTS
 2–4 fresh green chillies, seeded
 8 spring onions (scallions)
 2 garlic cloves, halved
 50g/2oz salted capers
 fresh tarragon sprig
 bunch of fresh parsley
 grated rind and juice of 1 lime
 juice of 1 lemon
 90ml/6 tbsp olive oil
 15ml/1 tbsp green Tabasco sauce
 ground black pepper

1 Put the chillies, spring onions and garlic in a food processor and pulse briefly until they are coarsely chopped.

2 Rub the salt off the capers. Add the capers and herbs to the food processor and pulse until very finely chopped.

3 Spoon the salsa into a bowl. Lightly stir in the lime rind and juice, lemon juice and oil. Add Tabasco and pepper. Cover and chill for up to 8 hours.

Habanero salsa

This is a fiery salsa. Habañero chillies, also called scotch bonnets, are very hot, whereas costeno amarillo chillies have a sharp citrus flavour, which harmonizes with the grapefruit or orange and lime.

MAKES ABOUT 250ML/8FL OZ/1 CUP

INGREDIENTS
 2 dried roasted habañero chillies
 2 dried costeno amarillo chillies
 2 spring onions (scallions),
  finely chopped
 juice of ½ large grapefruit or
  1 Seville (Temple) orange
 grated rind and juice of 1 lime
 small bunch of fresh
  coriander (cilantro)
 salt

1 Soak all the chillies in hot water for about 10 minutes, until softened. Drain, reserving the soaking water.

2 Remove the stalks from the chillies, then slit them and scrape out the seeds with a small, sharp knife. Put the chillies in a food processor, add a little of the reserved soaking liquid and then process to a fine paste. Spoon the chilli purée into a bowl.

3 Put the spring onions in another bowl and add the grapefruit or orange juice, then the lime rind and juice. Coarsely chop the coriander and add to the spring onions.

4 Add the coriander mixture to the chilli paste and mix thoroughly, then season to taste with salt. Cover and chill for at least one day before using.

Orange and chive salsa

Sweet oranges and fresh chives are teamed with rich tomato to make a tasty salsa, which is not at all spicy. This is a great one to serve with chicken tikka.

MAKES ABOUT 350ML/12FL OZ/1½ CUPS

INGREDIENTS
    2 large oranges
    1 beefsteak tomato
    bunch of fresh chives
    1 garlic clove, thinly sliced
    30ml/2 tbsp olive oil
    sea salt

1 Slice the bottom off one orange so that it will stand upright. Slice off the peel. Cut the orange into segments. Squeeze the membrane for any juice. Repeat with the second orange. Chop the segments, and add them to the bowl.

2 Halve the tomato and use a teaspoon to scoop the seeds into the bowl. Finely dice the flesh and add it to the bowl.

3 Use a pair of kitchen scissors to snip the chives into the bowl. Add the garlic slices. Pour on the olive oil, season with sea salt and stir. Serve within 2 hours.

Lime guacamole

An essential part of a Tex-Mex spread, enjoy this creamy avocado dip with corn chips or serve it as a cold sauce with chicken, fish or a juicy steak.

MAKES ABOUT 475ML/16FL OZ/2 CUPS

INGREDIENTS
    2 large ripe avocados
    1 small red onion, finely chopped
    1 fresh red or green chilli, seeded
      and very finely chopped
    1 garlic clove, crushed with salt
    finely shredded rind of ½ lime
    juice of 1½ limes
    pinch of caster (superfine) sugar
    225g/8oz tomatoes, seeded
      and chopped
    30ml/2 tbsp coarsely chopped fresh
      coriander (cilantro)
    15ml/1 tbsp olive oil
    salt and ground black pepper

1 Halve, stone (pit) and peel the avocados. Set one half aside. Chop the remaining halves and put them in a bowl. Mash coarsely with a fork.

2 Add the onion, chilli, garlic, lime rind and about two-thirds of the lime juice. Stir in the sugar, tomatoes and chopped coriander. Season with salt and pepper and add more lime juice to taste. Stir in the olive oil.

3 Dice the remaining avocado and stir it into the guacamole, then leave to stand for 15 minutes before serving.

COOK'S TIP
As well as adding a citrus zing, the lime juice helps prevent discoloration.

Pickled lemon and chilli dip

The piquancy of pickled lemons and the sweet bite of the chillies makes this a delicious dip for tortilla chips.

MAKES ABOUT 350ML/12FL OZ/1½ CUPS

INGREDIENTS
    200g/7oz soft (white farmer's) cheese
    30ml/2 tbsp double (heavy) or
      sour cream
    1 drained pickled lemon
    8 drained bottled Peppadew chillies
      (pickled cherry chillies)
    paprika, for dusting
    cucumber, carrot and celery sticks or
      tortilla chips, to serve

1 Put the soft cheese in a bowl and beat it until soft. Beat in the cream or sour cream.

2 Rinse the pickled lemon if it is still salty, then carefully scrape away the pulp, leaving the rind. Chop this finely. Chop the Peppadews to a similar size.

3 Stir the lemon and chillies into the cheese mixture, dust the surface lightly with paprika and serve with crudités or tortilla chips.

MARINADES AND STUFFINGS

Citrus juice makes an excellent basis for a marinade, since the acid is a valuable tenderizer. This is very useful when it comes to meat and poultry, but if you are marinating fish, keep the marinating time short or the fish may break up.

Citrus is also a very good ingredient in stuffings. Choose between the warm, sweet flavour of orange or mandarin, or the tartness of a lemon or lime.

Lemon and rosemary marinade

This is lovely with lamb for roasting. If used with chicken pieces, lift them out of the marinade before cooking, or the chicken could become tough.

MAKES ABOUT 350ML/12FL OZ/1½ CUPS

INGREDIENTS
    1 lemon, sliced
    6 fresh rosemary sprigs
    15ml/1 tbsp cornflour (cornstarch)
    150ml/¼ pint/⅔ cup lemon juice
    150ml/¼ pint/⅔ cup dry white wine
    60ml/4 tbsp olive oil
    salt and ground black pepper

1 Place your chosen meat in a large shallow pan or dish that will not react with the acid in the marinade. Sprinkle the lemon slices and rosemary on top.

2 Put the cornflour in a bowl and stir in enough of the lemon juice to make a paste. Stir in the remaining juice, with the wine, oil and a little salt and pepper. Pour over the meat, cover and leave for 4–6 hours, turning occasionally. Roast meat – but not poultry – in the marinade. If grilling the meat over a barbecue, use the marinade for basting.

Orange and green peppercorn marinade

A perfect marinade for fish. If a whole fish is used, you can afford to marinate it for up to 4 hours; marinate steaks or fillets for no more than 1 hour.

MAKES ABOUT 750ML/1¼ PINTS/3 CUPS

INGREDIENTS
    1 red onion, sliced
    2 small oranges, peeled and sliced
    90ml/6 tbsp mild olive oil
    30ml/1 tbsp cider vinegar
    30ml/2 tbsp drained green
      peppercorns in brine
    30ml/2 tbsp chopped fresh parsley
    salt and sugar

1 Slash a whole fish three or four times on either side. Line an ovenproof dish with foil. Lay half the onion and orange slices on the foil, place the whole fish or portions on top and cover with the remaining onion and orange slices.

2 Mix the remaining ingredients in a jug (pitcher) and pour them over the fish. Cover and set aside for up to 4 hours, depending on whether you are using portions or a whole fish. Bake the fish in the oven.

Lemon rub

This makes a marvellous dry marinade for chicken. Rub it on to the skin about 1 hour before roasting or grilling on the barbecue. You need to allow time to dry the lemon rind, so make this a few days before you intend to use it.

MAKES ABOUT 50G/2OZ

INGREDIENTS
    2 lemons
    30ml/2 tbsp chopped fresh
      lemon thyme
    15ml/1 tbsp chopped fresh
      lemon verbena
    15ml/1 tbsp chopped lemon grass

1 Peel the lemon in fine strips and then air-dry the rind and herbs on a rack in a warm place for up to two days.

2 When thoroughly dry, powder the lemon rind, using a pestle and mortar. Add the dried herbs and crush to blend together and make a powder.

COOK'S TIP
You can dry the lemon peel in an airing cupboard, if you have one, though a warm kitchen will do just as well.

Parsley, lemon and thyme stuffing

This is a very good stuffing to use with poultry. Slide it under the breast of a chicken before roasting it, or use it to stuff a poussin.

MAKES ABOUT 175G/6OZ

INGREDIENTS
  30g/1oz/2 tbsp butter
  1 small onion, finely chopped
  1 celery stick, finely chopped
  115g/4oz/2 cups fresh
    white breadcrumbs
  15ml/1 tbsp chopped fresh parsley
  10ml/2 tsp chopped fresh thyme
  grated rind of ½ lemon
  beaten egg, to bind
  salt and ground black pepper

1 Melt half the butter in a frying pan and cook the onion and celery over a low heat for about 5 minutes, or until the onion is tender. Remove from the heat and leave to cool.

2 Mix the breadcrumbs, parsley, thyme, and lemon rind in a small bowl. Add the onion mixture, the remaining butter, and enough of the egg to bind. Season with salt and pepper, and mix well.

Apricot and mandarin stuffing

An aromatic, golden mixture that makes the perfect stuffing for pork. Try it as a filling for pork fillet or tenderloin. Use the handle of a wooden spoon to make a hole right through the centre of the fillet, insert the stuffing and roast.

MAKES ABOUT 175G/6OZ

INGREDIENTS
  15g/½oz/1 tbsp butter
  1 small onion or leek, finely chopped
  115g/4oz/2 cups fresh white or
    wholemeal (whole-wheat)
    breadcrumbs
  50g/2oz/¼ cup ready-to-eat
    dried apricots
  6 mandarin segments, chopped
  grated rind of ½ orange
  beaten egg, to bind

1 Melt the butter in a frying pan and cook the onion or leek over a low heat for about 5 minutes, or until tender. Leave to cool.

2 Mix the breadcrumbs, dried apricots, mandarin segments and orange rind in a bowl. Add the onion with enough egg to bind. Season and mix well.

Prune, orange and nut stuffing

This makes enough to stuff a 4.5kg/10lb turkey, so amounts are generous. Reduce the quantities if you want to use it for a duck or chicken.

MAKES ABOUT 500G/1¼LB

INGREDIENTS
  115g/4oz/1 cup pitted prunes
  60ml/4 tbsp sherry
  25g/1oz/2 tbsp butter
  1 onion, finely chopped
  225g/8oz/4 cups fresh
    white breadcrumbs
  finely grated rind of 1 orange
  2 eggs, beaten
  30ml/2 tbsp chopped fresh parsley
  15ml/1 tbsp mixed dried herbs
  large pinch of ground allspice
  large pinch of freshly grated nutmeg
  115g/4oz/1 cup chopped walnuts
  2 celery sticks, finely chopped
  salt and ground black pepper

1 Put the prunes and sherry in a small pan. Cover and simmer gently until the prunes are tender. Remove from the heat and set aside to cool.

2 Melt the butter in a heavy frying pan and cook the onion over a low heat for about 5 minutes, or until it is softened. Remove the pan from the heat and leave to cool.

3 The prunes should have absorbed most, if not all, of the sherry. Cut each prune into four pieces. Place in a large bowl and add the onions. Stir in all the remaining ingredients, seasoning with salt and pepper. Use immediately, or cover and chill until needed.

CITRUS BUTTERS

Adding flavour to your food is easy when you top a steak, a succulent piece of white fish, chicken, or lamb chops with a pat of tangy citrus butter. If your sandwiches need updating, soften the citrus butter and use it to spread over the bread. Sweet butters are wonderful melted over waffles and pancakes too.

Maître d'hôtel butter

This is the classic parsley and lemon butter, frequently used for fish, but also great on steak or chops.

MAKES ABOUT 115G/4OZ/½ CUP

INGREDIENTS
   115g/4oz/½ cup unsalted (sweet)
      butter, at room temperature
   30ml/2 tbsp finely chopped
      fresh parsley
   2.5ml/½ tsp lemon juice
   cayenne pepper
   salt and ground black pepper

1 Put the butter into a mixing bowl and soften it by beating it with a spoon. Beat in the parsley, lemon juice and cayenne pepper. Season with salt and pepper.

2 Spread the butter 1cm/¼in thick on a piece of baking parchment, greaseproof (waxed) paper or foil. Chill until firm, then stamp out small rounds or other shapes using pastry (cookie) cutters.

3 If you want to make a butter roll, which can later be cut into slices, spoon the butter on to the foil or paper, then shape it, using the foil or paper as a guide. Do this as quickly as you can, as the heat from your hands will melt the butter. Wrap and chill.

Fennel and lime butter

Scallops taste sublime when teamed with this delectable butter. It also tastes wonderful on swordfish steaks. Only the feathery tops of the fennel are used, but don't waste the bulb – cut it into wedges and cook to serve with the fish.

MAKES ABOUT 225G/8OZ/1 CUP

INGREDIENTS
   1 fennel bulb, with plenty of
      feathery leaves
   2 egg yolks
   grated rind and juice of 1 lime
   175g/6oz/¾ cup butter
   salt and ground black pepper

1 Trim the feathery leaves from the fennel bulb and chop them finely.

2 Place the egg yolks in a bowl and whisk in the grated lime rind and juice. Continue to whisk until the mixture is pale and smooth.

3 Melt the butter in a pan. Gradually whisk it into the egg yolk mixture, until the sauce is thick and smooth. Add the chopped fennel leaves, salt and pepper to taste and stir well to mix.

Maître d'hôtel butter variations

These ideas are a good way of using up extra citrus. Use 115g/4oz/½ cup unsalted (sweet) butter.

Lemon and lime butter Add 15ml/1 tbsp finely grated lemon or lime rind and 15ml/1 tbsp juice. Omit the cayenne pepper.

Citrus butter Increase the lemon juice to 5ml/1 tsp or use 10ml/2 tsp orange juice or 5ml/1 tsp lime juice. Add the grated rind of 1 lemon, orange or lime. Omit the parsley and cayenne pepper.

Coriander-lime butter Omit the lemon juice, parsley and the cayenne pepper. Chop 25g/1oz/1 cup fresh coriander (cilantro). Mix into the butter with the grated rind and juice of 1 lime.

Sweet orange butter Instead of using lemon juice, add 10ml/2 tsp orange juice and the finely grated rind of 1 orange. Omit the parsley, cayenne pepper and seasoning. Sweeten it with 30ml/2 tbsp icing (confectioners') sugar.

CITRUS DRESSINGS

Although lemon is the juice most closely associated with dressings, other citrus juices can be used to delicious effect. Orange juice, for instance, works very well in a dressing that contains soy sauce, and grapefruit juice has an affinity for balsamic vinegar and virgin olive oil. Gremolata, a dry mixture of lemon rind, garlic and parsley, makes a tasty garnish sprinkled over stews.

Lemon vinaigrette

The original salad dressing for green leaves, this is often also called French dressing (except in France, that is). It is basically a mixture of oil and lemon juice, with extra ingredients that vary, depending on what kind of salad it is to be used for. Vinegar can be the acid element, but the ratio of oil to acid must be adjusted because vinegar has a stronger flavour than lemon. You can make it hours before you need it – just give it a quick whisk to bring it back up to scratch – but don't let green leaves sit in it for too long or they'll wilt. Some cooks mix vinaigrette by the jam-jar-full and keep it in the refrigerator, but it tastes infinitely better freshly made.

MAKES ABOUT 150ML/¼ PINT/⅔ CUP

INGREDIENTS
  1 garlic clove
  5ml/1 tsp Dijon mustard
  45–60ml/3–4 tbsp lemon juice
  150ml/¼ pint/⅔ cup good quality
    olive oil
  salt and ground black pepper

1 Put the garlic on a board, sprinkle it with a little salt and crush with the flat side of the blade of a cook's knife.

2 Scrape the crushed garlic into a small bowl and beat in the mustard, then the lemon juice.

3 Using a whisk (the horseshoe-shaped type works best), gradually whisk in the oil until the dressing thickens and emulsifies. Season to taste.

Grapefruit vinaigrette

Tangy and full of flavour, grapefruit juice makes an excellent salad dressing. Try it with romaine leaves or watercress.

MAKES ABOUT 150ML/¼ PINT/⅔ CUP

INGREDIENTS
  45ml/3 tbsp grapefruit juice
  10ml/2 tbsp balsamic vinegar
  5ml/1 tsp Provençal or red
    pepper mustard
  120ml/4fl oz/½ cup mild, fruity
    olive oil or a mixture of sunflower
    oil and extra virgin olive oil
  salt, ground black pepper and sugar

Mix the grapefruit juice and balsamic vinegar in a bowl. Whisk in the mustard and a pinch each of salt, pepper and sugar. Slowly whisk in the oil. Taste and adjust the seasoning if necessary.

Grapefruit and yogurt dressing

This oil-free dressing makes a healthy change from vinaigrette.

MAKES ABOUT 250ML/8FL OZ/1 CUP

INGREDIENTS
  30ml/2 tbsp pink grapefruit juice
  15ml/1 tbsp sherry vinegar
  1 garlic clove, crushed
  5ml/1 tsp wholegrain mustard
  150ml/¼ pint/⅔ cup natural (plain)
    low-fat yogurt
  15ml/1 tbsp chopped fresh herbs

Mix the grapefruit juice and vinegar in a bowl. Add the garlic, mustard, then whisk in the yogurt and herbs.

Gremolata

The traditional finishing flourish for the Milanese dish of osso buco. This makes enough for one stew, four lamb kebabs, four pork chops, or four portions of chunky white fish.

Grate 1 lemon. Crush 2 garlic cloves to a paste or chop very finely with salt. Chop a small bunch of parsley then mix with the lemon rind and garlic. Sprinkle over the food just before serving.

SAVOURY SAUCES

The most popular lemon-based sauce is mayonnaise, but because it does not have a strong citrus flavour, few people connect it with the fruit. Other sauces featuring citrus include orange butter sauce, Cumberland sauce and the famous Sauce bigarade.

Never-fail mayonnaise

The capital of the Balearic island of Minorca is almost certain to have lent its name to this famous sauce, when the French duc de Richelieu took the city of Mahon in 1756. Mayonnaise has many different uses, in sandwiches and hamburgers, as a salad dressing and as a sauce with fish and chicken. This version is made with a food processor for ease. Have all the ingredients at room temperature before you start.

MAKES ABOUT 350ML/12FL OZ/1½ CUPS

INGREDIENTS
   1 egg, plus 1 egg yolk
   5ml/1 tsp Dijon mustard
   juice of 1 large lemon
   175ml/6fl oz/¾ cup olive oil
   175ml/6fl oz/¾ cup rapeseed
     (canola), sunflower or corn oil
   salt and white pepper

1 Process the whole egg and yolk in a food processor for 20 seconds. Add the mustard, half the lemon juice, and a pinch of salt and pepper. Process for about 30 seconds until mixed.

2 With the motor running, pour in the oils through the feeder tube in a thin stream. Process until the mayonnaise is thick. Taste and add more lemon juice and seasoning if necessary.

Basil and lemon mayonnaise

This is delicious served with baked new potatoes or used as a dip for French fries. It also makes a great partner for lightly poached salmon.

MAKES ABOUT 350ML/12FL OZ/1½ CUPS

INGREDIENTS
   2 large (US extra large) egg yolks
   15ml/1 tbsp lemon juice
   150ml/¼ pint/⅔ cup mild olive oil
   150ml/¼ pint/⅔ cup sunflower oil
   a handful of fresh green basil leaves
   a handful of fresh opal basil leaves
   4 garlic cloves, crushed
   salt and ground black pepper

1 Place the egg yolks and lemon juice in a food processor or blender and process them briefly to mix. With the motor running, add the oils, slowly at first, then in a steady stream. Continue processing until the mixture forms a thick, creamy mayonnaise.

2 Tear both types of basil into pieces and stir them into the mayonnaise with the crushed garlic. Add salt and pepper to taste. Spoon into a serving bowl, cover and chill until ready to serve.

Tartare sauce

This is the real thing – tartare sauce made from scratch – but if you are short of time, you could always stir the flavourings into a good quality bought mayonnaise. It is perfect with fish.

MAKES 200ML/7FL OZ/SCANT 1 CUP

INGREDIENTS
   2 hard-boiled eggs
   1 egg yolk
   10ml/2 tsp lemon juice
   175ml/6fl oz/¾ cup olive oil
   5ml/1 tsp each chopped capers,
     gherkin, fresh chives and parsley
   salt and ground black pepper

1 Halve the hard-boiled eggs, scoop the yolks into a sieve placed over a bowl and push them through with the aid of a spoon. Stir in the raw egg yolk until smooth. Stir in the lemon juice.

2 Whisk in the oil, a little at a time. When the mixture starts to thicken, add the oil more quickly, so that it forms an emulsion. Finely chop one egg white (save the other for another dish) and stir it into the sauce with the capers, gherkin and herbs. Season to taste.

Avgolemono sauce

This frothy, light lemon mixture is the sauce version of a classic Greek recipe that is more often served as a soup. It tastes great with oily fish, such as sardines, with chicken or with a medley of roasted Mediterranean vegetables. Adjust the stock accordingly.

MAKES ABOUT 250ML/8FL OZ/1 CUP

INGREDIENTS
   10ml/2 tsp arrowroot
   grated rind and juice of
    1 large lemon
   120ml/4fl oz/½ cup vegetable,
    chicken or fish stock
   3 egg yolks

1 Put the arrowroot and lemon rind in a heavy pan. Strain the lemon juice, then add to the pan and mix thoroughly. Stir in the stock, then bring the mixture to the boil over a low heat, whisking constantly until smooth and thickened.

2 Remove the pan from the heat and add the egg yolks, whisking constantly. Return the pan to the heat and cook, still whisking constantly, for 1 minute. Serve immediately.

Hollandaise sauce

This classic sauce has a reputation for being quite difficult to make, as it will separate if it gets too hot. This version is much easier. Serve it with asparagus, artichokes, poached eggs (to make eggs Benedict), peas, broccoli, poached salmon and fish mousses.

MAKES ABOUT 300ML/½ PINT/1¼ CUPS

INGREDIENTS
   3 egg yolks
   15–30m/1–2 tbsp lemon juice
   175g/6oz/¾ cup unsalted (sweet)
    butter, diced
   salt and ground black pepper

1 Add the egg yolks and 15ml/1 tbsp of the lemon juice to a heavy pan. Season and whisk well to combine.

2 Add the butter and set the pan over a medium heat. Whisk constantly so that as the butter melts, it is blended into the egg yolks.

3 Continue whisking over a medium heat until the sauce is thick. Taste and add more lemon juice, salt and pepper if needed.

Simple sauce variations

Mayonnaise and hollandaise can be easily varied, with great results.
Aioli Add 4 garlic cloves with the eggs when making mayonnaise. Great as a dip for potato chunks, and superb with mussels.

Remoulade To 300ml/½ pint/ 1¼ cups mayonnaise, add 15ml/ 1 tbsp each of chopped fresh chives, tarragon and parsley, Dijon mustard and chopped, drained gherkins, and 5ml/1 tsp each of anchovy essence and chopped capers. Serve with braised celeriac.

Mousseline Add 150ml/¼ pint/ ⅔ cup of whipped cream to a cooled hollandaise sauce, and whisk well. Serve as a dip with artichoke hearts.
Sauce Maltaise Grate the rind from 1 blood orange, taking care to avoid the pith, and squeeze the juice from 2 blood oranges. Whisk the juice into warm hollandaise, then stir in the grated rind. Serve with cooked green vegetables.

Orange butter sauce

A simple sauce, this is wonderful tossed with wild mushrooms that have been fried in butter. Sprinkle over chopped fresh parsley and serve with toast.

MAKES ABOUT 350ML/12FL OZ/1½ CUPS

INGREDIENTS
 juice of 4 large oranges
 pinch of cayenne pepper
 175g/6oz/¾ cup unsalted (sweet)
  butter, diced
 salt

1 Pour the orange juice into a small, heavy pan and bring to the boil. Boil until the liquid has reduced to about 30ml/2 tbsp. Add salt and cayenne pepper to taste.

2 Over a low heat, gradually whisk in the butter, piece by piece, to produce a creamy and smooth sauce. It is best if each piece of butter is fully incorporated before adding the next cube. Serve the sauce immediately.

COOK'S TIP
Use unsalted butter as its sweeter flavour is more suited to this sauce.

Cumberland sauce

This British classic is served with a hot piece of gammon or ham, cold game or tongue, and is good brushed over lamb for the last few minutes of cooking.

MAKES ABOUT 475ML/16FL OZ/2 CUPS

INGREDIENTS
 1 unwaxed lemon
 1 unwaxed orange
 2 sugar cubes
 150ml/¼ pint/⅔ cup port
 4 allspice berries
 4 cloves
 5ml/1 tsp mustard seeds
 225g/8oz redcurrant jelly
 10ml/2 tsp arrowroot
 30ml/2 tbsp orange liqueur
 pinch of ground ginger

1 Pare the lemon, avoiding the pith. Snip or cut the peel into thin strips.

2 Put the lemon rind in a pan, cover with water and bring to the boil. Cook for 5 minutes, drain and set aside.

3 Wash the orange, then rub it all over with the sugar cubes, until they are saturated with the citrus oil.

4 Pour the port into a small pan and add the sugar cubes and whole spices. Bring to the boil, then leave to cool. Strain the port into a pan, add the jelly and stir over a low heat until dissolved.

5 Mix the arrowroot with the orange liqueur and stir it into the sauce. Bring the sauce to the boil and cook gently for 1–2 minutes until thickened.

6 Remove from the heat and add the lemon rind and ground ginger. Cool to room temperature before serving.

COOK'S TIP
To develop a rich flavour, store this sauce in the refrigerator for a few days then bring to room temperature before serving.

Orange and caper sauce

Fish gets the luxury treatment with this sweet-and-sour sauce. It is classically served with poached skate, but tastes just as good with an oily fish such as mackerel. Adding the fish bones and trimmings will give the sauce depth.

MAKES ABOUT 475ML/16FL OZ/2 CUPS

INGREDIENTS
  25g/1oz/2 tbsp butter
  1 onion, chopped
  fish bones and trimmings
  5ml/1 tsp black peppercorns
  300ml/½ pint/1¼ cups dry
    white wine
  2 small oranges
  15ml/1 tbsp drained capers
  60ml/4 tbsp crème fraîche
  salt and ground black pepper

1 Melt the butter in a pan and sauté the onion over a medium heat until it is lightly browned. Add the fish trimmings and peppercorns, then pour in the wine. Cover and simmer for 30 minutes.

2 Using a sharp knife, peel the oranges. Working over a bowl, ease the segments away from the membranes.

3 Strain the stock into a clean pan. Add the capers and orange segments, with any juice. Heat through. Reduce the heat to the lowest setting and stir in the crème fraîche. Season and serve hot.

Sauce bigarade

The classic orange sauce to serve with duck and rich game.

MAKES ABOUT 550ML/18FL OZ/2½ CUPS

INGREDIENTS
  roasting pan juices or 25g/1oz/
    2 tbsp butter
  40g/1½oz/3 tbsp plain
    (all-purpose) flour
  300ml/½ pint/1¼ cups hot stock
  150ml/¼ pint/⅔ cup red wine
  2 unwaxed Seville (Temple) oranges
    or 2 sweet oranges plus 10ml/2 tsp
    lemon juice
  15ml/1 tbsp orange liqueur
  30ml/2 tbsp redcurrant jelly
  salt and ground black pepper

1 Pour off any excess fat from the roasting pan, leaving the juices, or melt the butter in a small pan. Add the flour and cook, stirring constantly, for about 4 minutes, or until lightly browned.

2 Remove from the heat and gradually blend in the stock and wine. Bring to the boil, stirring constantly. Lower the heat and simmer gently for 5 minutes.

3 Meanwhile, using a zester, pare the rind thinly from one orange. Squeeze the juice from both oranges.

4 Blanch the rind by putting it in a pan, pouring over boiling water to cover and cooking for 5 minutes. Drain the rind then return it to the pan. Add the sauce to the pan.

5 Add the orange juice and lemon juice to the pan, if using, with orange liqueur and redcurrant jelly, stirring to dissolve the jelly. Season to taste and serve.

SWEET SAUCES

One of the many reasons that makes citrus so special is its affinity for both sweet and savoury dishes. In sweet sauces, citrus really stars.

Lemon custard

This creamy sauce is perfect spooned over a steamed lemon sponge pudding, or poured over the sponges in a trifle. It is also delicious with sliced bananas.

MAKES ABOUT 600ML/1 PINT/2½ CUPS

INGREDIENTS
  15ml/1 tbsp cornflour (cornstarch)
  15ml/1 tbsp custard powder (see Cook's tip)
  15ml/1 tbsp caster (superfine) sugar
  finely grated rind of 2 lemons
  600ml/1 pint/⅔ cup milk
  15g/½oz/1 tbsp butter

1 Mix the cornflour and custard powder in a large bowl. Stir in the sugar and lemon rind.

2 Stir in 15–30ml/1–2 tbsp of the milk and mix to a paste. Heat the remaining milk in a pan. As soon as bubbles start to appear on the surface, around the edge, remove the pan from the heat.

3 Gradually stir the hot milk into the paste, until the mixture is very smooth. Return it to the pan and heat gently, stirring until thick. Whisk in the butter to finish.

COOK'S TIP

If you cannot find custard powder use cornflour (cornstarch) instead. The colour will not be so bright, but the flavour will not be compromised.

Orange honey sauce

This is a quick and easy sauce to make. Try it over hot pancakes or waffles for a delicious dessert.

MAKES ABOUT 300ML/½ PINT/1¼ CUPS

INGREDIENTS
  175ml/6fl oz/¾ cup clear honey
  50g/2oz/¼ cup butter
  50g/2oz/⅓ cup muscovado (molasses) sugar
  grated rind and juice of 2 large oranges

Mix all the ingredients in a heavy pan. Place over a low heat and stir constantly until the sugar has dissolved and the sauce is warm.

Sabayon

Serve this sauce hot over a steamed pudding or chill as described and serve just as it is with dessert cookies. Never let it stand, as it will collapse.

MAKES ABOUT 250ML/8FL OZ/1 CUP

INGREDIENTS
  1 egg
  2 egg yolks
  75g/3oz/⅔ cup caster (superfine) sugar
  150ml/¼ pint/⅔ cup sweet white wine
  grated rind and juice of 1 lemon

1 Whisk the egg, yolks and sugar until they are pale and thick.

2 Stand the bowl over a pan of hot water. Add the wine and lemon juice, a little at a time, whisking vigorously. Continue whisking until the mixture leaves a trail from the whisk. Whisk in the lemon rind. If serving hot, serve immediately.

3 To serve cold, place over a bowl of iced water and whisk until chilled. Pour into small glasses and serve at once.

Hot orange and red wine sauce

This tangy sauce has a vibrant colour. It looks and tastes great with fruit pies, and is also good with crêpes.

MAKES ABOUT 300ML/½ PINT/1¼ CUPS

INGREDIENTS
    4 oranges, such as Valencia
    250ml/8fl oz/1 cup fruity red wine
    25g/1oz/2 tbsp soft light brown sugar
    1 cinnamon stick
    2 cloves
    5ml/1 tsp cornflour (cornstarch)
    15ml/1 tbsp water or orange liqueur, such as Cointreau or Grand Marnier
    25g/1oz/2 tbsp butter, diced

1 Using a zester, thinly pare the rind from half an orange and place it in a small pan. Squeeze the juice from all the oranges and strain it into the pan. Add the wine, brown sugar, cinnamon stick and cloves. Heat until the sugar has completely dissolved, then simmer for 10 minutes until reduced.

2 Mix the cornflour with the water or liqueur in a small cup. Add to the red wine mixture and simmer for 1 minute, until slightly thickened.

3 Remove and discard the cloves and cinnamon stick and gradually whisk in the butter, one piece at a time until smooth and glossy. Make sure each piece is incorporated before adding more. Serve immediately.

Orange, lemon or lime crème pâtissière

This is also known as pastry cream, which gives a clue to its most common use. Spread it in a cold baked pastry case (pie shell) and top with kiwi fruit and mandarin segments, then add an orange glaze for a sophisticated treat. It is a good idea to make the custard the day before you need it, so that it can be thoroughly chilled.

MAKES ABOUT 300ML/½ PINT/1¼ CUPS

INGREDIENTS
    3 egg yolks
    50g/2oz/¼ cup caster (superfine) sugar
    1 orange, lemon or lime
    40g/1½oz/6 tbsp plain (all-purpose) flour
    250ml/8fl oz/1 cup milk
    1 vanilla pod (bean), split lengthways

1 In a heatproof bowl, whisk the egg yolks with the sugar until pale. Finely grate the orange, lemon or lime directly into the bowl or, if easier, grate onto a sheet of baking parchment and then add to the egg mixture. Sift over the flour and whisk it in.

2 Pour the milk into a small pan and add the vanilla pod. Bring to the boil, remove the vanilla pod and slowly pour the hot milk over the egg mixture, whisking constantly.

3 Pour the mixture into a heavy pan and return the vanilla pod. Bring to the boil, lower the heat and gently simmer for 2 minutes, stirring constantly with a wooden spoon, until thickened. Transfer the mixture to a bowl and cover closely with clear film (plastic wrap). Leave to cool, then chill until needed.

Citrus cream

The simplest sauce of all, this flavoured whipped cream is very good with a rich sweet pie and adds an extra boost to a plate of mixed summer berries.

MAKES 300ML/½ PINT/1¼ CUPS

INGREDIENTS
    300ml/½ pint/1¼ cups double (heavy) cream
    5ml/1 tsp icing (confectioners') sugar
    grated rind of 1 lemon, 1 orange or 1 lime

Whip the cream to soft peaks with a small balloon whisk or electric mixer. Add the icing sugar and grated citrus rind and beat until the cream holds its shape. Transfer to a serving dish and serve immediately.

CITRUS DRINKS

Orange, lemon and lime go well in many drinks, but grapefruit can also be used for colour and flavour.

THIRST QUENCHERS

These home-made drinks are cooling, but without the cloying sweetness or additives typical of commercial drinks.

Old-fashioned lemonade

The traditional drink for a long summer, this is best enjoyed in a hammock after a vigorous game of tennis.

SERVES TWO

INGREDIENTS
　2 lemons
　75g/3oz/6 tbsp caster
　　(superfine) sugar
　2 egg whites
　300ml/½ pint/1¼ cups boiling water
　75ml/5 tbsp sherry (optional)
　ice cubes

1 Pare a few strips of rind from one of the lemons, and add to a pan. Cut both lemons in half and squeeze the juice.

2 Strain the juice to remove any pips, then add to the pan containing the rind.

3 Add the sugar and egg whites and whisk until frothy. Whisk in the water. Continue to whisk for 2 minutes more, until the sugar has dissolved. Pour in the sherry, if using, a little at a time, whisking after each addition.

4 To serve, put several ice cubes into tall glasses, pour over the lemonade, and decorate with mint, if you like.

Orange and raspberry smoothie

This combines the fragrant flavour of raspberries and the tang of citrus with creamy yogurt – a perfect way to start the day or a great pick-me-up when your energy begins to flag.

SERVES THREE

INGREDIENTS
　250g/9oz/about 2 cups
　　raspberries, chilled
　200ml/7fl oz/scant 1 cup natural
　　(plain) yogurt
　300ml/½ pint/1¼ cups freshly
　　squeezed orange juice, chilled

1 Put the chilled raspberries and yogurt in a food processor or blender and process for 1 minute to make a smooth and creamy purée. Reserve a few raspberries for decoration.

2 Add the orange juice to the raspberry and yogurt mixture and process for about 30 seconds, or until thoroughly combined and smooth.

3 To serve, pour into tall glasses and decorate with a few whole raspberries. Serve immediately with a swizzle stick for stirring, if you like.

Citrus shake

It would be hard to find a drink with more flavour and zest than this mix of three citrus and pineapple.

SERVES FOUR

INGREDIENTS
　1 pineapple
　3 grapefruit, using 1 each white,
　　pink and ruby grapefruit
　2 oranges, peeled and chopped
　juice of 1 lemon

1 To prepare the pineapple, cut the bottom and the top off the fruit. Stand the pineapple upright and cut off the skin, removing all the spikes, but taking off as little of the flesh as possible. Cut the flesh into bitesize chunks.

2 Peel and segment the grapefruit, removing the membrane, if you wish. Put in a food processor or blender along with the pineapple, oranges and lemon juice. Process until combined.

3 Press the fruit juice through a sieve to remove any pith or membranes. Pour into tall glasses and serve the shakes chilled, with straws, if you wish.

HOT CITRUS DRINKS

Adding a slice or two of orange, lemon or lime to mulled wine or hot coffee is a great way to bring out their flavour and is wonderfully aromatic.

Mulled wine

The perfect way to welcome guests on a chilly winter evening.

SERVES FOUR

INGREDIENTS
    70cl bottle red wine
    75g/3oz/6 tbsp soft light brown sugar
    2 cinnamon sticks
    1 lemon, sliced
    4 whole cloves
    150ml/¼ pint/⅔ cup brandy or port
    lemon slices, to serve

1 Put all the ingredients, except the brandy or port, into a large pan. Bring to the boil, then remove from the heat. Cover and leave to stand for 5 minutes, to allow the flavours to infuse (steep).

2 Strain the liquid into a heatproof bowl, to remove the spices and lemon slices. Add the brandy or port. Serve warm, decorated with a half slice of lemon.

Café brûlot

This mixture of coffee, brandy and orange liqueur, with pared citrus rinds, makes a spectacular drink when flamed at the table.

SERVES FOUR TO SIX

INGREDIENTS
    1 orange
    1 lemon
    30ml/2 tbsp caster (superfine) sugar
    6 cloves
    1 cinnamon stick
    175ml/6fl oz/¾ cup brandy
    45–60ml/3–4 tbsp Curaçao or other
      orange liqueur
    475ml/16fl oz/2 cups hot strong
      black coffee
    4–6 cinnamon and orange rind twists

1 Pare the rind of the orange and the lemon in one strip and place in a pan.

2 Add the sugar, cloves, cinnamon, brandy and liqueur, and heat to dissolve the sugar. Have the hot coffee ready. Carefully ignite the brandy mixture, then add the coffee in a steady stream. Serve in heatproof glasses, decorated with a cinnamon stick and orange rind twist.

Café à l'orange

Sip this drink slowly and savour the contrast between the thick citrus cream topping and hot liqueur coffee beneath.

SERVES FOUR

INGREDIENTS
    120ml/4fl oz/½ cup whipping or
      double (heavy) cream
    30ml/2 tbsp icing
      (confectioners') sugar
    5ml/1 tsp grated orange rind
    600ml/1 pint/2½ cups hot strong
      black coffee
    150ml/¼ pint/⅔ cup orange liqueur
    4 orange wedges, to decorate

1 Whip the cream until stiff, then fold in the icing sugar and orange rind. Chill for 30 minutes, or until the flavoured cream is firm enough to support a wedge of orange.

2 Divide the hot black coffee equally among four tall glass mugs and stir about 30ml/2 tbsp liqueur into each. Top with a generous swirl of the chilled whipped cream, then place an orange wedge on the cream. Serve immediately, sipping the drink through the cream.

CITRUS COCKTAILS

Ever since their heyday in the 1920s and 1930s, cocktails have been very popular, and continue to be so today. Citrus is a favourite ingredient, whether juiced, sliced or rubbed around the rim of a glass to provide a tart tingle as a prelude to the drink itself.

Harvey wallbanger

Galliano has a wonderful affinity for orange juice, as this extremely popular cocktail demonstrates.

SERVES ONE

INGREDIENTS
    30ml/2 tbsp vodka
    15ml/1 tbsp Galliano liqueur
    150ml/¼ pint/⅔ cup orange juice
    crushed ice
    1 small orange, to decorate

1 Pour the spirits and juice into a tall glass or cocktail shaker full of crushed ice. Mix or shake the cocktail for about 30 seconds to chill it.

Bartender's tips

Freshly squeezed orange juice or bottled fresh orange juice is one of the most important elements in drinks based on single spirit shots, particularly with the white spirits such as gin, vodka and white rum. In cocktails, freshly squeezed lemon juice is great for cutting through the sweetness of many liqueurs. Fresh lime juice is even sourer, and is used in drinks that demand a powerful tang.

2 Use a canelle knife (zester) to take strips of rind off the orange. Cut the orange into thin, even slices.

3 Cut the orange slices in half and sit them between cracked ice in a highball glass. Strain the cocktail into the glass, decorate with the rind and serve.

Morning glory fizz

Despite the name, it's not necessary to drink this first thing in the morning.

SERVES ONE

INGREDIENTS
    15ml/1 tbsp brandy
    5ml/1 tsp orange Curaçao
    5ml/1 tsp lemon juice
    1 dash anisette
    2 dashes Angostura bitters
    soda water (club soda), to taste
    twist of lemon rind, to decorate

Pour the brandy, Curaçao, lemon juice and anisette into a cocktail shaker filled with crushed ice and shake for about 20 seconds. Strain into a small, chilled cocktail glass. Add bitters to taste and top up the glass with soda water. Decorate with the lemon twist.

Tequila sunset

Try this recipe for a different take on a tequila sunrise. For that drink, bright red grenadine sinks to the bottom and then blends upwards into the orange juice. Here, the orange, tequila and crème de cassis represent a glowing sunset sky above a honeyed horizon.

SERVES ONE

INGREDIENTS
    30ml/2 tbsp tequila
    120ml/4fl oz/½ cup lemon
    juice, chilled
    40ml/1½ tbsp orange juice, chilled
    30ml/2 tbsp clear honey
    15ml/1 tbsp crème de cassis

1 Pour the tequila and then the lemon and orange juices straight into a tall, well-chilled cocktail glass.

2 Mix the ingredients by twisting a swizzle stick between the palms of your hands. Drizzle the honey into the glass so that it falls in a layer at the bottom.

3 Add the crème de cassis – but don't stir – to add a glowing layer above the honey in the glass.

Gin and lemon fizz

The citrus sorbet here is enhanced by pretty ice cubes, filled with curls of pared lemon rind, berries or flowers.

SERVES TWO

INGREDIENTS
  berries and currants
  pieces of thinly pared lemon and
    orange rind
  tiny edible flowers, such as rose
  4 scoops lemon sorbet (sherbet)
  30ml/2 tbsp gin
  120ml/4fl oz/½ cup tonic water

1 To make the ice cubes, place a mixture of fruit, pared rind and flowers in separate sections of an ice cube tray.

2 Carefully fill with water and freeze for several hours until solid. Divide the sorbet between two glasses. Pour over the gin and add a couple of the ice cubes to each glass. Top up with tonic water and serve.

VARIATION
Substitute orange sorbet for the lemon, sparkling mineral water for the tonic and add 30ml/2 tbsp Cointreau with the gin.

Iced citrus Margarita

This smooth, cooling tangy sorbet drink has all the punch of Mexico's renowned cocktail. Serve in tall, slim glasses.

SERVES TWO

INGREDIENTS
  30ml/2 tbsp lime juice
  30ml/2 tbsp caster (superfine) sugar,
    plus extra for frosting
  4 lime and 4 lemon slices
  60ml/4 tbsp tequila
  30ml/2 tbsp Cointreau
  6–8 small scoops of orange or lime
    sorbet (sherbet)
  150ml/¼ pint/⅔ fizzy lemonade

1 Frost the glasses, using lime juice and sugar. Carefully add two lime and two lemon slices to each glass, standing them on end.

2 Mix the tequila, Cointreau and lime juice in a bowl. Scoop the sorbet into the glasses, pour the tequila mixture over and top up with the lemonade.

VARIATION
Frost the rims of the glasses with salt instead of sugar, for a traditional taste.

Snowball

Lime, nutmeg and ice cream give this cocktail an irresistible smooth and very creamy taste.

SERVES FOUR

INGREDIENTS
  8 scoops vanilla ice cream
  120ml/4fl oz/½ cup advocaat
  60ml/4 tbsp lime juice
  freshly grated nutmeg
  300ml/½ pint/1¼ cups chilled
    fizzy lemonade

1 Put half the vanilla ice cream in a food processor or blender and add the advocaat and the lime juice, with plenty of freshly grated nutmeg. Process the mixture briefly until well combined.

2 Scoop the remaining ice cream into four glasses. Pour over the advocaat mixture and top up the glasses with lemonade. Sprinkle with more nutmeg.

Quick citrus cocktails
Milano Mix equal measures of gin and Galliano liqueur with crushed ice and the juice of ¼ lemon in a cocktail shaker. Shake, then strain into a cocktail glass.
Gimlet Stir equal measures of Plymouth gin and lime cordial in a glass with a couple of ice cubes.
Gin rickey Half-fill a tall glass with ice. Add 45ml/3 tbsp gin, the juice of ¼ lime or ¼ lemon and a generous dash of grenadine. Stir vigorously, then top with fresh soda water (club soda).

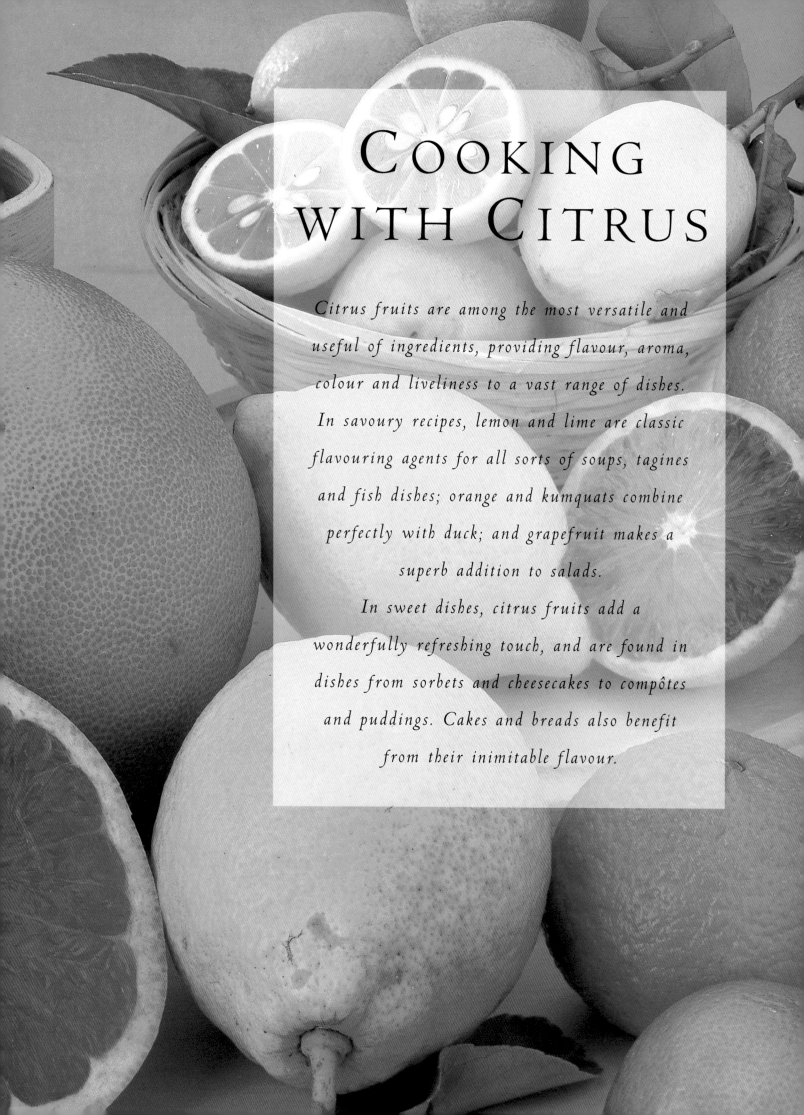

COOKING WITH CITRUS

Citrus fruits are among the most versatile and useful of ingredients, providing flavour, aroma, colour and liveliness to a vast range of dishes. In savoury recipes, lemon and lime are classic flavouring agents for all sorts of soups, tagines and fish dishes; orange and kumquats combine perfectly with duck; and grapefruit makes a superb addition to salads.

In sweet dishes, citrus fruits add a wonderfully refreshing touch, and are found in dishes from sorbets and cheesecakes to compôtes and puddings. Cakes and breads also benefit from their inimitable flavour.

SOUPS AND APPETIZERS

*Fragrant soups and zesty appetizers are a delicious way
to start any meal, and the refreshing sharpness of citrus fruit is
perfect to cleanse the palate and stimulate the appetite.
Recipes range from chickpea, lemon and parsley soup to ricotta
fritters with avocado salsa. There are also more exotic dishes such as
Thai fish broth and butterflied Mediterranean prawns, all with the
special tangy flavour that comes from citrus fruit.*

CHICKPEA, LEMON AND PARSLEY SOUP

LEMON ENHANCES THE FLAVOUR OF FRESH PARSLEY IN THIS TASTY NORTH AFRICAN INSPIRED SOUP,
WHICH MAKES A SUBSTANTIAL LUNCH SERVED WITH MOROCCAN OR CRUSTY BREAD.

2 Place the onion and parsley in a food processor or blender and process until finely chopped.

3 Heat the mixed oils in a large frying pan and gently cook the onion mixture for about 4 minutes over a low heat, or until slightly softened.

4 Add the chickpeas, cook gently for about 2 minutes, then add the stock. Season well with salt and pepper. Bring the soup to the boil, then cover and simmer for 20 minutes, or until the chickpeas are very tender.

5 Leave the soup to cool a little and then part-purée in a food processor or blender, or mash the chickpeas fairly coarsely with a fork, so that the soup is thick, but still quite chunky.

SERVES SIX

INGREDIENTS
   225g/8oz/1¼ cups chickpeas,
     soaked overnight
   1 small onion, coarsely chopped
   1 bunch fresh parsley (about
     40g/1½oz/1½ cups)
   30ml/2 tbsp olive oil and sunflower
     oil, mixed
   1.2 litres/2 pints/5 cups
     chicken stock
   juice of ½ lemon
   salt and ground black pepper
   lemon wedges and thinly pared
     and shredded lemon rind,
     to garnish
   crusty bread, to serve

1 Drain the chickpeas and rinse well under cold running water. Cook them in rapidly boiling water for 10 minutes, then simmer for 1–1½ hours, or until tender. Drain and, using your fingertips, gently peel away the skins.

6 Return the soup to a clean pan, stir in the lemon juice, then taste and adjust the seasoning, if necessary. Heat it through gently, then serve, garnished with lemon wedges and shredded lemon rind, and accompanied by crusty bread.

THAI FISH BROTH

LIMES, LEMON GRASS, CHILLIES AND GALANGAL ARE AMONG THE FLAVOURINGS USED IN THIS FRAGRANT SOUP. IT LOOKS AND TASTES DELICIOUS, AND WOULD BE THE PERFECT CHOICE FOR A DINNER PARTY.

SERVES TWO TO THREE

INGREDIENTS

1 litre/1¾ pints/4 cups fish or light
  chicken stock
4 lemon grass stalks
3 limes
2 small fresh hot red chillies, seeded
  and thinly sliced
2cm/¾in piece fresh galangal or
  ginger, peeled and thinly sliced
6 coriander (cilantro) stalks
2 kaffir lime leaves, coarsely chopped
  (optional) (see Cook's Tip)
350g/12oz monkfish fillet,
  membrane removed and cut into
  2.5cm/1in pieces
15ml/1 tbsp rice vinegar
45ml/3 tbsp Thai fish sauce
30ml/2 tbsp chopped coriander
  (cilantro) leaves, to garnish

1 Pour the stock into a heavy pan and bring it to the boil over a medium heat. Meanwhile, slice the bulb end of each lemon grass stalk diagonally into pieces about 3mm/⅛in thick.

2 Peel off four wide strips of lime rind with a vegetable peeler, taking care to avoid the white pith underneath which would make the soup bitter. Squeeze the limes and reserve the juice.

3 Add the sliced lemon grass, strips of lime rind, chillies, galangal or ginger slices and coriander stalks to the stock, with the kaffir lime leaves, if using. Simmer for 1–2 minutes.

COOK'S TIP

If you use kaffir lime leaves, you will need the juice of only 2 limes.

4 Add the monkfish, rice vinegar and Thai fish sauce, with half the reserved lime juice. Simmer for about 3 minutes, or until the fish is just cooked. Lift out and discard the coriander stalks, taste the broth and add more lime juice, if necessary; the soup should taste quite sour. Sprinkle with the coriander leaves and serve very hot.

RICOTTA FRITTERS WITH AVOCADO SALSA

THE FRESH-FLAVOURED SALSA SPIKED WITH A LITTLE RED ONION, CHILLI AND LIME IS EXCELLENT WITH THESE MELT-IN-THE-MOUTH HERBED SPRING ONION FRITTERS.

MAKES ABOUT TWELVE

INGREDIENTS
  250g/9oz/generous 1 cup
    ricotta cheese
  1 large (US extra large) egg, beaten
  90ml/6 tbsp self-raising
    (self-rising) flour
  90ml/6 tbsp milk
  1 bunch spring onions (scallions),
    thinly sliced
  30ml/2 tbsp chopped fresh
    coriander (cilantro)
  sunflower oil, for shallow frying
  salt and ground black pepper
  fresh coriander (cilantro) sprigs and
    lime wedges, to garnish
  200ml/7fl oz/scant 1 cup crème
    fraîche, to serve
For the salsa
  225g/8oz tomatoes
  2 ripe, but not soft, avocados
  1 small red onion, diced
  grated rind and juice of 1 lime
  ½–1 fresh green or red chilli, seeded
    and finely chopped
  30–45ml/2–3 tbsp chopped mixed
    fresh mint and coriander (cilantro)
  pinch of caster (superfine) sugar
  5–10ml/1–2 tsp Thai fish sauce

1 First, make the salsa. Peel and seed the tomatoes and roughly dice the flesh. Peel, stone (pit) and dice the avocados. Place in a small bowl with the onion, lime rind and juice. Add chilli to taste, the tomatoes, mint and coriander. Season with salt, pepper, sugar and Thai fish sauce. Mix well and set aside for about 30 minutes.

2 Beat the ricotta until smooth, then beat in the egg and flour, followed by the milk to make a smooth, thick batter. Beat in the spring onions and coriander. Season well with pepper and a little salt.

3 Heat a little oil in a non-stick frying pan over a medium heat. Add spoonfuls of the mixture to make fritters about 7.5cm/3in across, and fry for 5 minutes each side, or until set and browned. The mixture makes about 12 fritters.

4 Taste the salsa and adjust the seasoning, adding more sugar to taste. Serve the ricotta fritters immediately, with the salsa and a spoonful of crème fraîche. Garnish with coriander sprigs and lime wedges.

VARIATION
The fritters are also excellent served with thinly sliced smoked salmon.

CITRUS FISHCAKES <u>WITH</u> CUCUMBER RELISH

THESE WONDERFUL, SMALL FISHCAKES ARE A VERY FAMILIAR AND POPULAR APPETIZER IN THAILAND AND INCREASINGLY THROUGHOUT SOUTH-EAST ASIA. THEY ARE USUALLY SERVED WITH CHILLED BEER.

MAKES ABOUT TWELVE

INGREDIENTS
  3 kaffir lime leaves, plus extra
    to garnish
  300g/11oz cod fillet, cut into chunks
  30ml/2 tbsp red curry paste
  1 egg
  30ml/2 tbsp Thai fish sauce
  5ml/1 tsp sugar
  30ml/2 tbsp cornflour (cornstarch)
  15ml/1 tbsp chopped fresh
    coriander (cilantro)
  50g/2oz green beans, thinly sliced
  vegetable oil, for frying
For the cucumber relish
  60ml/4 tbsp rice or coconut vinegar
  50g/2oz/¼ cup sugar
  1 head pickled garlic
  15ml/1 tbsp chopped fresh
    root ginger
  1 cucumber, cut into thin batons
  4 shallots, thinly sliced

1 First, make the cucumber relish. Place the vinegar and sugar in a small pan with 60ml/4 tbsp water and bring to the boil, stirring constantly until the sugar has dissolved. Set aside to cool.

2 Separate the head of pickled garlic into individual cloves. Chop these finely and place in a bowl with the ginger. Add the cucumber and shallots, stir, then add to the vinegar mixture and mix well.

3 Thinly slice the kaffir lime leaves. Put the chunks of fish, curry paste and egg in a food processor and process to a smooth paste.

4 Transfer the mixture to a small bowl and stir in the Thai fish sauce, sugar, cornflour, sliced kaffir lime leaves, coriander and green beans. Mix well, then shape the mixture into 12 or more cakes, measuring about 5mm/¼in thick and 5cm/2in in diameter.

5 Heat the oil in a wok or deep frying pan. Fry the fishcakes, a few at a time, for about 4–5 minutes, or until cooked and evenly brown.

6 Lift out the fishcakes and drain them on kitchen paper. Keep each batch hot while frying successive batches. Garnish with the extra kaffir lime leaves and serve with the cucumber relish.

BUTTERFLIED MEDITERRANEAN PRAWNS

SKEWERED PRAWNS, MARINATED IN A FIERY HERB AND LIME DRESSING, THEN GRILLED UNTIL PINK AND TENDER, MAKE A DELICIOUS FIRST COURSE OR LIGHT LUNCH.

SERVES FOUR

INGREDIENTS
  32 raw king prawns (jumbo shrimp)
  2 garlic cloves, finely chopped
  90ml/6 tbsp finely chopped
    fresh parsley
  1 fresh rosemary sprig, leaves
    removed and finely chopped
  pinch of dried chilli flakes
  juice of 2 limes
  30ml/2 tbsp olive oil
  salt and ground black pepper
  green salad, to serve

1 Wash the prawns in salted water and remove their heads and shells. Make a shallow cut down the centre of the curved back of each prawn. Pull out the black vein with the point of a knife or a cocktail stick (toothpick).

2 To butterfly the prawns, cut more deeply along the deveining cut, without completely cutting through them, then carefully fan out.

3 Blend the garlic, parsley, rosemary, chilli flakes, lime juice and olive oil in a large bowl. Stir in the prawns, season and leave to marinate for 1 hour.

4 Meanwhile, soak 32 wooden skewers in warm water for at least 30 minutes.

5 Preheat the grill (broiler) until very hot. Thread two prawns on to each pair of skewers and grill (broil) for about 2 minutes, or until each side has turned pink. Remove the prawns from the skewers and serve with green salad.

SEARED SCALLOPS WITH LEMON AND THYME

TENDER SCALLOPS NEED VERY LITTLE COOKING. THEY ARE DELICIOUS MARINATED WITH THYME AND GARLIC AND COOKED WITH LEMON AND BALSAMIC VINEGAR. THE CURVED TOP SHELLS MAKE ATTRACTIVE DISHES FOR SERVING — MAKE SURE THEY ARE WELL SCRUBBED FIRST.

SERVES FOUR

INGREDIENTS
  50ml/2fl oz/¼ cup olive oil
  2 garlic cloves, finely chopped
  4 fresh thyme sprigs
  1 bay leaf
  15ml/1 tbsp chopped fresh parsley
  16 fresh scallops, prepared and rinsed
  1 shallot, finely chopped
  15ml/1 tbsp balsamic vinegar
  30ml/2 tbsp lemon juice
  150ml/¼ pint/⅔ cup chicken or
    vegetable stock
  salt and ground black pepper
  24 baby spinach leaves, to garnish

1 Blend the olive oil, garlic, thyme, bay leaf and parsley in a shallow bowl. Add the scallops and leave to marinate in a cool place for 1 hour.

2 Heat a large, heavy frying pan until it smokes. Remove the scallops from the marinade and drain well. Add them to the pan and sear for about 30 seconds on each side until they turn opaque. This will seal in their juices, but do not overcook them or they will become tough. Transfer the scallops to a plate and keep warm.

3 Add the marinade to the pan, then add the shallot, balsamic vinegar, lemon juice and stock. Cook over a high heat for 5 minutes. Discard the bay leaf and season well.

4 Neatly arrange six spinach leaves around each scallop shell in the centre of each of four serving plates. Place four scallops on each shell and pour over the juices. Serve immediately.

COOK'S TIP
To prepare the scallops, use a sturdy, short-bladed knife to prise the shell apart. Scrape away the fringe next to the edible white and orange (coral) part, and remove the intestinal thread. Remove the edible part. Retain four shells for serving. If you prefer, buy shelled scallops and serve in small dishes.

SEARED SWORDFISH WITH CITRUS DRESSING

THE JAPANESE TRY OUT NEW DISHES FROM ALL OVER THE WORLD AND THEN ARRANGE THEM IN A
TRADITIONAL WAY. THIS SALAD IS A GOOD EXAMPLE OF THAT PRACTICE. FRESH FISH IS SLICED THINLY
AND SEARED, THEN SERVED WITH CRISP SALAD VEGETABLES WITH A LIME DRESSING.

SERVES FOUR

INGREDIENTS
75g/3oz mooli (daikon), peeled
50g/2oz carrot, peeled
1 cucumber
10ml/2 tsp vegetable oil
300g/11oz skinned fresh swordfish
 steak, cut against the grain
2 cartons mustard and cress
15ml/1 tbsp toasted sesame seeds
For the dressing
105ml/7 tbsp shoyu
105ml/7 tbsp water mixed with
 5ml/1 tsp dashi-no-moto
30ml/2 tbsp toasted sesame oil
juice of ½ lime
rind of ½ lime, shredded into strips

1 Use a very sharp knife, mandolin or vegetable slicer with a julienne blade to make very thin (4cm/1½in long) strands of mooli, carrot and cucumber. Soak the mooli and carrot in iced water for about 5 minutes, then drain and chill.

2 To make the dressing, mix together all the ingredients in a small bowl. Stir well, then chill.

3 Heat the oil in a frying pan until smoking hot. Sear the fish for about 30 seconds on all sides. Immediately plunge it into cold water in a bowl to stop the cooking. Gently pat dry on kitchen paper and wipe off as much oil as possible.

4 Using a sharp knife, cut the swordfish steak in half lengthways before slicing it into 5mm/¼in thick pieces in the opposite direction, against the grain.

5 Arrange the fish slices in a ring on individual dinner plates. Mix together the vegetable strands, mustard and cress and sesame seeds. Fluff up with your hands, then shape them into four spheres. Gently place each sphere in the centre of the plate, on top of the swordfish. Pour the dressing around the plate's edge and serve immediately.

COOK'S TIPS
• Dashi-no-moto are freeze-dried granules that are used to make a quick dashi stock. They are available from Japanese supermarkets and some other specialist stores.
• This dish is traditionally made with fillet cut with the grain. To prepare, cut it in half lengthways, then slice against the grain by holding a knife horizontally to the chopping board.

CEVICHE <u>WITH</u> RED ONION, AVOCADO <u>AND</u> SWEET POTATO

MARINATING FISH IN CITRUS JUICE HAS A SIMILAR EFFECT TO COOKING, MAKING THE FISH OPAQUE AND FIRM. KNOWN AS CEVICHE, THIS DISH IS A TRADITIONAL SOUTH AMERICAN ONE, AND HERE IT IS COMBINED WITH SWEET POTATOES, AVOCADOS AND PRAWNS TO MAKE A DELICIOUS SALAD.

SERVES SIX

INGREDIENTS
- 500–675g/1¼–1½lb white fish fillets, skinned
- 1 red onion, thinly sliced
- pinch of dried red chilli flakes
- grated rind of 1 small lime and juice of 5 limes
- 450–500g/1–1¼lb sweet potatoes, unpeeled
- 75ml/5 tbsp mild olive oil
- 15–25ml/1–1½ tbsp rice vinegar
- 2.5–5ml/½–1 tsp caster (superfine) sugar
- 2.5ml/½ tsp ground toasted cumin seeds
- ½–1 fresh red or green chilli, seeded and finely chopped
- 1 large or 2 small avocados, peeled, stoned (pitted) and sliced
- 225g/8oz cooked peeled prawns (shrimp)
- 45ml/3 tbsp chopped fresh coriander (cilantro)
- 30ml/2 tbsp roasted peanuts, chopped
- salt and ground black pepper

1 Cut the fish into strips or chunks. Sprinkle half the onion over the base of a glass dish and lay the fish on top. Sprinkle on the dried red chilli flakes and pour in the lime juice. Cover and chill for 2–3 hours, spooning the lime juice over the fish once or twice. Drain, and discard the onion.

2 Steam or boil the sweet potatoes for 20–25 minutes, or until just tender. Peel and slice, or cut into wedges.

3 Place the oil in a bowl and whisk in the rice vinegar and sugar to taste, then add the cumin, season, and whisk in the fresh chilli and grated lime rind.

4 In a glass bowl, toss the fish, sweet potatoes, avocado slices, prawns and most of the coriander with the dressing.

5 Add the remaining half of the sliced red onion and toss to mix. Sprinkle over the remaining coriander and the peanuts and serve immediately.

POULTRY AND MEAT DISHES

The tangy sharpness of citrus fruit is the perfect foil for rich meat and poultry dishes, whether in a classic combination, such as chicken and salad, or in an unfamiliar guise, such as ham with a fruity clementine sauce. By contrast, it is also ideal for adding zest and piquancy to lighter meats, such as chicken and veal, that can sometimes seem rather bland and unexciting. Citrus fruit is so versatile that it can be used as a single, keynote flavouring, in a subtle partnership with garlic and herbs, or as part of a blend with aromatic spices to give depth and variety to every kind of meat and poultry.

TURKEY PATTIES WITH LIME

MINCED TURKEY, DELICATELY FLAVOURED WITH LIME AND THYME, MAKES DELICIOUSLY LIGHT PATTIES, WHICH ARE IDEAL FOR EASY, MIDWEEK MEALS. SERVE THE PATTIES IN SPLIT AND TOASTED BUNS OR PIECES OF CRUSTY BREAD, WITH CHUTNEY, SALAD LEAVES AND CHUNKY FRIES.

SERVES SIX

INGREDIENTS

675g/1½lb minced (ground) turkey
1 small red onion, finely chopped
grated rind and juice of 1 lime
small handful of fresh thyme leaves
15–30ml/1–2 tbsp olive oil
salt and ground black pepper

VARIATIONS

• Minced (ground) chicken, lamb, pork or beef could be used instead of turkey in these patties.
• You could try chopped oregano, parsley or basil in place of the thyme, and lemon rind instead of lime.

1 Mix together the turkey, onion, lime rind and juice, thyme and seasoning. Cover and chill for up to 4 hours to allow the flavours to infuse (steep), then divide the mixture into six equal portions and shape into round patties.

2 Preheat a griddle pan. Brush the patties with oil, then cook them on the griddle for 10–12 minutes. Turn them over, brush with more oil and cook for 10–12 minutes on the second side, or until cooked through. Serve hot.

TEX-MEX BURGERS <u>WITH</u> LIME GUACAMOLE

MELT-IN-THE-MOUTH GUACAMOLE WITH ITS DISTINCTIVE FLAVOURS OF CHILLI, GARLIC AND LIME, IS THE PERFECT ACCOMPANIMENT TO THESE EASY TEX-MEX BURGERS. SERVE THE BURGERS IN WARMED CORN TORTILLAS FOR A FABULOUS HAND-HELD MEAL.

SERVES FOUR

INGREDIENTS
   500g/1¼lb lean minced
     (ground) beef
   1 small onion, finely chopped
   1 small green (bell) pepper, seeded
     and finely chopped
   1 garlic clove, crushed
   oil, for brushing
   4 fresh tortillas
   salt and ground black pepper
   chopped fresh coriander (cilantro),
     to garnish
   salad, to serve
For the lime guacamole
   2 ripe avocados
   1 garlic clove, crushed
   2 tomatoes, chopped
   juice of 1 lime
   ½ green chilli, seeded and chopped
   30ml/2 tbsp chopped fresh coriander

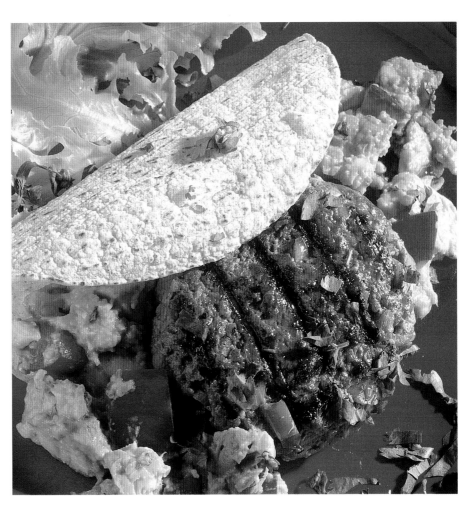

1 Put the minced beef, onion, green pepper and garlic in a bowl and mix well. Season with salt and pepper.

2 Using your hands, shape the mixture into four large, round burgers and brush them with oil.

COOK'S TIP
The guacamole should be made not more than an hour before it is needed, or it will start to brown. If it has to be left to stand, sprinkle a little extra lime juice over the top and stir just before serving.

3 To make the lime guacamole, cut the avocados in half, remove the stones (pits) and scoop out the flesh.

4 Put in a bowl and mash the avocado flesh roughly. Add the garlic, tomatoes, lime juice, chilli and coriander and mix well. Season with salt and pepper.

5 Cook the burgers on a medium hot barbecue or under the grill (broiler) for 10 minutes, turning once. Heat the tortillas on the barbecue or under the grill for 15 seconds each side and then place some guacamole in the middle and add a burger to each. Garnish with coriander and serve with salad.

DUCK <u>WITH</u> CUMBERLAND SAUCE

THIS COMBINATION OF DUCK AND ORANGE IS SO GOOD IT SHOULDN'T BE RESERVED FOR SPECIAL OCCASIONS ONLY. SERVE WITH POTATOES AND PEAS FOR A SIMPLE, BUT DELICIOUS, WEEKDAY MEAL.

SERVES EIGHT

INGREDIENTS
    4 minneolas or oranges, segmented,
        with rind and juice reserved
    2 × 2.25kg/5lb oven-ready ducks,
        with giblets
    salt and ground black pepper
    fresh parsley sprig, to garnish
For the Cumberland sauce
    30ml/2 tbsp plain (all-purpose) flour
    300ml/½ pint/1¼ cups chicken or
        duck stock
    150ml/¼ pint/⅔ cup port or red wine
    15ml/1 tbsp redcurrant jelly

1 Preheat the oven to 180°C/350°F/ Gas 4. Tie the minneola or orange rind with string and place it inside the cavities of the two ducks.

2 Place the ducks on a rack in one large or two smaller roasting pans, prick the skin well with a fork or a skewer, season with salt and pepper and cook for 30 minutes per every 450g/1lb (about 2½ hours) until the flesh is tender and the juices run clear.

3 Halfway through the cooking time, pour off the fat from the roasting pan(s) into a heatproof bowl. When the ducks are cooked, transfer them to a carving board, remove the orange rind from the cavities and reserve.

4 To make the sauce, remove any fat from the roasting pan(s), leaving the sediment and juices behind. If using two pans, scrape the sediment and juices into one of them. Sprinkle in the flour and cook over a low heat, stirring constantly, for 2 minutes.

VARIATION
Bigarade sauce is also classically served with duck, but is time-consuming to make. For a speedy version, thinly pare the rinds of 4 Seville (Temple) oranges, cut into thin strips and simmer in a pan of water for 10 minutes, then drain. Squeeze the juice from the oranges. Add the rind and juice in step 5 with the stock, but substitute red Bordeaux wine for the port and lemon juice for the redcurrant jelly. Stir in 5ml/1 tsp tomato purée (paste) and omit the orange segments.

5 Finely chop the reserved orange rind and add to the roasting pan with the stock, port or red wine and redcurrant jelly. Stir well to blend, then bring to the boil and simmer, stirring frequently, for about 10 minutes, then strain into a pan. Add the orange segments with their juices.

6 To carve the ducks, remove the legs and wings, cutting through the joints. Cut the two end joints off the wings and discard them. Cut the breast meat off the carcass in one piece and slice it thinly. Arrange the slices on a warmed serving plate with the legs and the wing joints. Spoon over a little of the hot sauce and serve the rest separately, in a sauce boat. Garnish with parsley and serve immediately.

COOK'S TIP
Cumberland sauce is extremely versatile and can be served with game, ham and mutton, although the latter is rarely available nowadays. It also goes very well with roast goose and turkey.

CITRUS CHICKEN SALAD

THIS LIGHT, ZESTY SALAD MAKES A REFRESHING CHANGE FROM RICH FOOD. IT IS A GOOD CHOICE FOR A POST-CHRISTMAS BUFFET, WHEN COOKED TURKEY CAN BE USED INSTEAD OF CHICKEN.

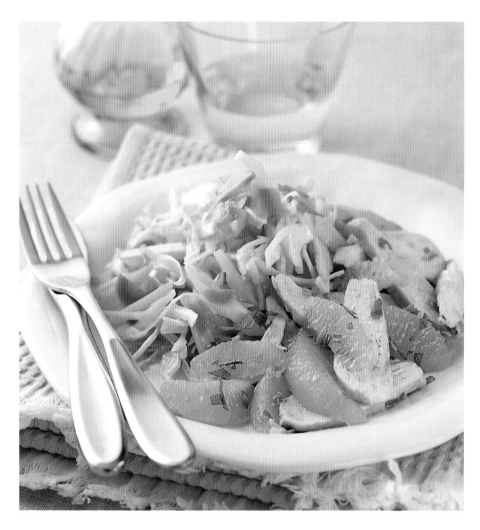

2 Using a sharp knife, cut a thin slice of peel and pith from each end of two of the oranges. Place them cut side down on a plate and cut off the peel and pith in strips. Remove any bits of remaining pith. Cut out each segment leaving the membrane behind and set aside. Grate the rind and squeeze the juice from one of the remaining oranges and place both in a large bowl.

3 Stir in the Dijon mustard, 5ml/1 tsp of the honey, 60ml/4 tbsp of the oil and seasoning to taste. Mix in the cabbage, carrots, spring onions and celery, then leave to stand for 10 minutes.

4 Meanwhile, squeeze the juice from the remaining orange and mix it with the tarragon and remaining honey and oil. Peel and segment the limes, as for the oranges, and lightly mix the lime segments into the dressing with the reserved orange segments. Season to taste with salt and pepper.

SERVES SIX

INGREDIENTS
   120ml/4fl oz/½ cup extra virgin
      olive oil
   6 skinless, boneless chicken
      breast portions
   4 oranges
   5ml/1 tsp Dijon mustard
   15ml/3 tsp clear honey
   300g/11oz/2¾ cups finely shredded
      white cabbage
   300g/11oz carrots, peeled and
      thinly sliced
   2 spring onions (scallions),
      thinly sliced
   2 celery sticks, cut into thin batons
   30ml/2 tbsp chopped fresh tarragon
   2 limes
   salt and ground black pepper

1 Heat 30ml/2 tbsp of the oil in a large, heavy frying pan. Add the chicken breast portions to the pan and cook for 15–20 minutes, or until the chicken is cooked through and golden brown. (If your pan is too small, cook the chicken in two or three batches.) Remove the chicken from the pan and leave to cool.

5 Thinly slice the cooled chicken portions and add them to the dressing. Spoon the vegetable salad on to six individual plates and add the chicken mixture, then serve immediately.

COOK'S TIP
Seedless navel oranges would be a good choice for this dish, but you could also use easy-to-peel Jaffa or Shamouti oranges or even substitute clementines, satsumas or ortaniques. As most varieties of tangerines are smaller than oranges, you will need five or six of them.

FRAGRANT THAI CHICKEN CURRY

LIMES REALLY BRING OUT THE THAI FLAVOURINGS IN THIS CREAMY CURRY. IT IS QUITE SIMPLE TO MAKE EVEN THOUGH IT INCLUDES A VARIETY OF UNUSUAL INGREDIENTS.

SERVES SIX

INGREDIENTS
  400ml/14oz can unsweetened
    coconut milk
  6 skinless, boneless chicken breast
    portions, thinly sliced
  225g/8oz can bamboo shoots,
    drained and sliced
  30ml/2 tbsp Thai fish sauce
  15ml/1 tbsp soft light brown sugar
For the green curry paste
  4 fresh green chillies, seeded
  1 lemon grass stalk, sliced
  1 small onion, sliced
  3 garlic cloves
  1cm/½in piece galangal or fresh root
    ginger, peeled and chopped
  grated rind of ½ lime
  5ml/1 tsp coriander seeds
  5ml/1 tsp cumin seeds
  2.5ml/½ tsp Thai fish sauce
To garnish
  1 fresh red chilli, seeded
  pared rind of ½ lime
  fresh Thai purple basil or
    coriander (cilantro)
To serve
  175g/6oz/scant 1 cup Thai
    jasmine rice
  pinch of saffron threads
  salt

1 First make the green curry paste. Put the chillies, lemon grass, onion, garlic cloves, galangal or ginger, lime rind, coriander seeds, cumin seeds and fish sauce in a food processor or blender and process until they are reduced to a thick, smooth paste.

2 Bring half the coconut milk to the boil in a large frying pan, then reduce the heat and simmer gently for about 5 minutes, or until reduced by half. Stir in the green curry paste and simmer for a further 5 minutes.

3 Add the sliced chicken to the pan and pour in the remaining coconut milk. Add the bamboo shoots, Thai fish sauce and sugar. Stir well to combine all the ingredients and bring the curry back to simmering point, then simmer gently for about 10 minutes, or until the chicken slices are cooked through. The mixture will look quite grainy or curdled during cooking, but do not worry, as this is quite normal.

4 To make the garnish, cut the chilli, lime rind and basil or coriander into fine strips. Add the rice and saffron to a pan of salted boiling water. Simmer for about 10 minutes, drain, then serve it with the curry and the prepared garnish.

CIDER-GLAZED HAM WITH CLEMENTINE AND CRANBERRY SAUCE

THIS WONDERFUL CURED HAM GLAZED WITH CIDER IS TRADITIONALLY SERVED WITH CRANBERRY SAUCE FLAVOURED WITH CLEMENTINES, AND IS IDEAL FOR ANY SPECIAL OCCASION MEAL. THERE ARE MANY DIFFERENT VARIETIES OF CIDER AVAILABLE – CHOOSE A DRY ONE FOR A LIGHT, CRISP TASTE.

SERVES EIGHT TO TEN

INGREDIENTS
  2kg/4½lb middle gammon (cured
    ham) joint
  1 large or 2 small onions
  about 30 whole cloves
  3 bay leaves
  10 black peppercorns
  1.3 litres/2¼ pints/5⅔ cups
    medium-dry (hard) cider
  45ml/3 tbsp soft light brown sugar
  bunch of fresh flat leaf parsley,
    to garnish (optional)
For the cranberry sauce
  350g/12oz/3 cups cranberries
  175g/6oz/¾ cup soft light
    brown sugar
  grated rind and juice of
    2 clementines
  30ml/2 tbsp port

1 Weigh the ham and calculate the cooking time, allowing 20 minutes per 450g/1lb, then place it in a flameproof casserole or pan. Stud the onion or onions with 5–10 of the cloves and add to the casserole or pan with the bay leaves and peppercorns.

2 Add 1.2 litres/2 pints/5 cups of the cider and enough water to just cover the ham. Heat until simmering and then carefully skim off the scum that rises to the surface, using a large spoon or ladle. Start timing the cooking from the moment the stock begins to simmer.

3 Cover with a lid or foil, and simmer gently for the calculated time. Towards the end of the cooking time, preheat the oven to 220°C/425°F/Gas 7.

4 Heat the sugar and remaining cider in a pan, stirring until the sugar has completely dissolved.

5 Simmer for 5 minutes to make a dark, sticky glaze. Remove the pan from the heat and set aside to cool for about 5 minutes.

COOK'S TIPS
• A large stock pot or preserving pan can be used for cooking the ham.
• Leave the ham until it is cool enough to handle before removing the hard rind. Snip off the string using a sharp knife or scissors, then carefully slice off the rind, leaving a thin, even layer of fat. Use a narrow-bladed, sharp knife for the best results – a filleting knife, or a long, slim ham knife would be ideal.

6 Lift out the ham. Slice off the rind to leave a thin layer of fat, then score the fat into a diamond pattern. Place the ham in a roasting pan.

7 Press a clove into the centre of each diamond. Spoon over the glaze and bake for 25 minutes, or until golden.

8 Gently simmer the sauce ingredients in a pan for about 20 minutes, stirring frequently. Serve the ham with the sauce, garnished with parsley, if you like.

FISH AND SHELLFISH

Pan-fried fish garnished with slices or wedges of lemon is almost a culinary cliché — although no less delicious for that — and is a clear indication of the perfect affinity between fish and citrus fruits. Freshly squeezed juice makes tangy marinades, and including slices of lemon, lime or orange in oven-baked fish parcels is one of the easiest ways to add extra flavour and piquancy. Adding fruit, rind or juice to fish and shellfish stews and curries balances both richness and spiciness. Fish is a popular choice for the health-conscious, and cooking it with citrus fruits is the ideal way of preventing its delicate flesh from drying out without the addition of oil, butter or other fats.

GREEN FISH CURRY

ANY FIRM-FLESHED FISH CAN BE USED FOR THIS DELICIOUS CURRY, WHICH GAINS ITS RICH FLAVOUR FROM A MIXTURE OF FRESH HERBS, SPICES AND LIME. EXOTIC FISH, SUCH AS MAHI-MAHI, HOKI OR SWORDFISH, OR HUMBLER FISH, SUCH AS COLEY, ALL WORK WELL.

SERVES FOUR

INGREDIENTS

4 garlic cloves, coarsely chopped
5cm/2in piece fresh root ginger,
  peeled and coarsely chopped
2 fresh green chillies, seeded and
  coarsely chopped
grated rind and juice of 1 lime
5–10ml/1–2 tsp shrimp
  paste (optional)
5ml/1 tsp coriander seeds
5ml/1 tsp Chinese
  five-spice powder
75ml/6 tbsp sesame oil
2 red onions, finely chopped
900g/2lb hoki fillets, skinned
400ml/14fl oz/1⅔ cups canned
  coconut milk
45ml/3 tbsp Thai fish sauce
50g/2oz/2 cups fresh coriander
  (cilantro) leaves
50g/2oz/2 cups fresh basil leaves
6 spring onions (scallions),
  coarsely chopped
150ml/¼ pint/⅔ cup sunflower or
  groundnut (peanut) oil
sliced fresh green chilli and finely
  chopped fresh coriander (cilantro),
  to garnish
cooked basmati or Thai fragrant rice
  and lime wedges, to serve

1 First make the curry paste. Combine the garlic, ginger, chillies, lime juice and shrimp paste, if using, in a food processor. Add the spices, with half the sesame oil. Process to a paste, then spoon into a bowl, cover and set aside.

2 Heat a wok or large, shallow pan, and pour in the remaining sesame oil. When it is hot, stir-fry the red onions over a high heat for 2 minutes. Add the fish and stir-fry for 1–2 minutes to seal the fillets on all sides.

3 Lift out the red onions and fish with a slotted spoon and put them on a plate. Add the curry paste to the wok or pan and fry for 1 minute, stirring constantly.

4 Return the hoki fillets and onions to the pan, pour in the coconut milk and bring to the boil. Lower the heat, add the Thai fish sauce and simmer gently for 5–7 minutes until the fish is cooked through and tender.

5 Meanwhile, process the herbs, spring onions, lime rind and sunflower or groundnut oil to a coarse paste in a food processor. Stir into the fish curry. Garnish with chilli and coriander and serve with rice and lime wedges.

COD CARAMBA

LIME ADDS SHARPNESS TO THE FRESH FLAVOURS IN THIS COLOURFUL MEXICAN DISH, WITH ITS CONTRASTING CRUNCHY TOPPING AND TENDER FISH FILLING.

SERVES FOUR TO SIX

INGREDIENTS
   2 tomatoes
   450g/1lb cod fillets
   225g/8oz smoked cod fillets
   300ml/½ pint/1¼ cups fish stock
   50g/2oz/¼ cup butter
   1 onion, sliced
   2 garlic cloves, crushed
   1 green (bell) pepper, seeded
     and diced
   1 red (bell) pepper, seeded and diced
   2 courgettes (zucchini), diced
   115g/4oz/⅔ cup drained canned or
     thawed frozen corn kernels
   juice of 1 lime
   Tabasco sauce
   salt, ground black pepper and
     cayenne pepper
For the topping
   75g/3oz tortilla chips
   50g/2oz/½ cup grated
     Cheddar cheese
   coriander (cilantro) sprigs, to garnish
   lime wedges, to serve

1 Plunge the tomatoes into boiling water for 30 seconds, then refresh in cold water. Peel off the skins, remove the seeds and chop the flesh. Set aside.

2 Lay the fish in a shallow pan and pour over the fish stock. Bring to the boil, lower the heat, cover and poach for about 8 minutes, or until the flesh flakes easily when tested with the tip of a sharp knife. Leave to cool slightly, then remove the skin and separate the flesh into large flakes. Keep hot.

3 Melt the butter in a pan, add the onion and garlic and cook over a low heat, stirring frequently, for 5 minutes until soft. Add the diced peppers, stir and cook for 2 minutes. Stir in the courgettes and cook for 3 minutes more, until the vegetables are tender.

4 Stir in the corn and tomatoes, then add lime juice and Tabasco sauce to taste. Season with salt, black pepper and cayenne. Cook for a couple of minutes to heat the corn and tomatoes, then stir in the fish and transfer to a dish that can safely be used under the grill (broiler).

VARIATION
This dish can also be made with other white fish such as haddock.

5 Preheat the grill. Make the topping by crushing the tortilla chips with a rolling pin, then mix in the cheese. Add cayenne pepper to taste and sprinkle over the fish. Place the dish under the grill until the topping is crisp and brown. Garnish with coriander sprigs and lime wedges and serve immediately.

THAI PRAWN SALAD WITH GARLIC DRESSING AND FRIZZLED SHALLOTS

IN THIS INTENSELY FLAVOURED SALAD, SWEET PRAWNS AND FRESH MANGO ARE PARTNERED WITH A SWEET-SOUR LIME AND GARLIC DRESSING ACCENTUATED WITH THE HOT TASTE OF CHILLI. THE CRISP FRIZZLED SHALLOTS ARE A TRADITIONAL ADDITION TO THAI SALADS.

SERVES FOUR TO SIX

INGREDIENTS

  675g/1½lb medium-size raw
    prawns (shrimp)
  finely shredded rind of 1 lime
  ½ fresh red chilli, seeded and
    finely chopped
  30ml/2 tbsp olive oil, plus extra
    for brushing
  1 ripe but firm mango
  2 carrots, cut into long,
    thin shreds
  10cm/4in piece cucumber, sliced
  1 small red onion, halved and
    thinly sliced
  a few sprigs of fresh
    coriander (cilantro)
  a few sprigs of fresh mint
  45ml/3 tbsp roasted peanuts,
    coarsely chopped
  4 large shallots, thinly sliced and
    fried until crisp in 30ml/2 tbsp
    groundnut (peanut) oil
  salt and ground black pepper
For the dressing
  1 large garlic clove, chopped
  10–15ml/2–3 tsp caster
    (superfine) sugar
  juice of 2 limes
  15–30ml/1–2 tbsp Thai fish sauce
  1 fresh red chilli, seeded
  5–10ml/1–2 tsp light rice vinegar

1 Peel the prawns and remove the heads, but leave the tails intact. Make a shallow cut down the centre of the curved back of each prawn. Pull out the black vein with the point of a cocktail stick (toothpick) or the tip of the knife, then rinse the prawns thoroughly in cold water.

COOK'S TIP
Removing the vein that runs along the back of prawns (shrimp) is to prevent it from spoiling the flavour. It is not toxic or dangerous.

2 Place the prawns in a glass or china dish and add the lime rind and chilli. Season with salt and pepper and spoon the oil over them. Toss to mix, cover with clear film (plastic wrap) and leave to marinate for 30–40 minutes.

3 To make the dressing, place the chopped garlic in a mortar with 10ml/2 tsp caster sugar and pound with a pestle until smooth, then gradually work in the juice of 1½ limes and about 15ml/1 tbsp of the Thai fish sauce.

4 Transfer the dressing to a small jug (pitcher). Finely chop half the red chilli and add it to the dressing. Taste the dressing and add more sugar, lime juice, Thai fish sauce and rice vinegar to taste.

5 Cut the mango in two either side of the stone (pit). Trim any flesh from the stone. Peel the remaining pieces and cut the flesh into very fine strips.

6 Put the mango, carrots, cucumber and onion and half the dressing in a large bowl and toss thoroughly to mix. Arrange the salad on individual plates or in bowls.

7 Heat a ridged, cast-iron griddle pan or heavy frying pan until very hot. Brush with a little oil, then sear the prawns for 2–3 minutes on each side, until they turn pink and are patched with brown on the outside. Arrange the prawns on the salads.

8 Sprinkle the remaining dressing over the salads and then sprinkle with the sprigs of coriander and mint. Finely shred the remaining chilli and sprinkle it over the salads with the peanuts and crisp-fried shallots. Serve immediately.

SPICED FISH BARBECUED THAI-STYLE

THAI SPICES AND LIME FLAVOUR RED MULLET OR SNAPPER, WHICH IS THEN WRAPPED IN BANANA LEAVES AND COOKED ON THE BARBECUE. IT MAKES A TASTY AND COLOURFUL MAIN COURSE. HOWEVER, IF BANANA LEAVES ARE NOT AVAILABLE, USE A DOUBLE LAYER OF FOIL INSTEAD.

SERVES FOUR

INGREDIENTS

4 red mullet or snapper, about
  350g/12oz each
banana leaves
1 lime
1 garlic clove, thinly sliced
2 spring onions (scallions),
  thinly sliced
30ml/2 tbsp Thai red curry paste
60ml/4 tbsp coconut milk

1 Scale the fish by holding the tail and scraping the scales away from the tail, using a knife. Slit the belly below the head and remove the guts. Rinse thoroughly under cold water.

2 Cut several deep slashes in the side of each fish with a sharp knife. Place each fish on a layer of banana leaves.

3 Thinly slice half the lime and tuck the slices into the slashes in the fish, with slivers of garlic. Sprinkle the spring onions over the fish.

4 Grate the rind and squeeze the juice from the remaining half-lime and mix with the curry paste and coconut milk. Spoon over the fish.

5 Wrap the leaves over the fish to enclose them completely. Tie firmly with kitchen string and cook on a medium-hot barbecue for about 15–20 minutes.

ASIAN FISH EN PAPILLOTE

THE AROMATIC SMELL THAT WAFTS OUT OF THESE FISH PARCELS AS YOU OPEN THEM IS DELICIOUSLY TEMPTING. LIME IS INCLUDED IN THE ASIAN FLAVOURINGS, WHICH PERFECTLY COMPLEMENT THE SUBTLE TASTE OF SALMON.

SERVES FOUR

INGREDIENTS
  2 courgettes (zucchini)
  2 carrots
  6 spring onions (scallions)
  2.5cm/1in piece fresh root
    ginger, peeled
  1 lime
  2 garlic cloves, thinly sliced
  30ml/2 tbsp Thai fish sauce
  5–10ml/1–2 tsp clear sesame oil
  4 salmon fillets, about 200g/
    7oz each
  ground black pepper
  rice, to serve

VARIATION
Thick fillets of hake, halibut, hoki and fresh or undyed smoked haddock and cod can all be used for this dish.

1 Slice the courgettes, carrots and spring onions into batons and set aside. Cut the root ginger into batons and put them in a bowl. Using a zester, pare the lime. Add the pared rind and garlic to the ginger. Squeeze the lime juice.

2 Place the fish sauce into a bowl and stir in the lime juice and sesame oil.

3 Preheat the oven to 220°C/425°F/ Gas 7. Cut out four rounds of baking parchment, with a diameter of 40cm/ 16in. Season the fish with pepper. Lay a fillet on one side of each paper round, about 3cm/1¼in off centre. Sprinkle a quarter of the ginger mixture over each and pile a quarter of the vegetable batons on top. Spoon a quarter of the Thai fish sauce mixture over the top.

4 Fold the bare side of the baking parchment over the salmon and roll the edges of the parchment over to seal each parcel very tightly.

5 Place the salmon parcels on a baking sheet and cook for about 10 minutes, depending on the thickness of the fillets. Put the parcels on plates and serve with rice.

VEGETARIAN AND VEGETABLE DISHES

Cuisines around the world have been quick to exploit the natural affinity between citrus fruits and vegetables, combining ingredients such as peppers, mushrooms, broccoli and asparagus with lemons, limes, oranges and grapefruit. Citrus fruits, in combination with herbs and spices, breathe new life into otherwise dull pulses, while pasta and rice dishes take on a completely new identity. These fruits also play an important role in vegetarian nutrition, as the presence of vitamin C enables the body to absorb the mineral iron from vegetable sources, which it otherwise couldn't do.

LEMONY COUSCOUS SALAD

*THIS IS A POPULAR SALAD OF OLIVES, ALMONDS AND COURGETTES MIXED WITH FLUFFY COUSCOUS
AND DRESSED WITH HERBS, LEMON JUICE AND OLIVE OIL. IT HAS A DELICATE FLAVOUR AND MAKES
AN EXCELLENT ACCOMPANIMENT TO GRILLED CHICKEN OR KEBABS.*

SERVES FOUR

INGREDIENTS

275g/10oz/1⅔ cups couscous
550ml/18fl oz/2½ cups boiling
  vegetable stock
2 small courgettes (zucchini)
16–20 black olives
25g/1oz/¼ cup flaked (sliced)
  almonds, toasted
60ml/4 tbsp olive oil
15ml/1 tbsp lemon juice
15ml/1 tbsp chopped fresh
  coriander (cilantro)
15ml/1 tbsp chopped fresh parsley
good pinch of ground cumin
good pinch of cayenne pepper

1 Place the couscous in a bowl and
pour over the boiling stock. Stir with
a fork and then set aside for 10 minutes
for the stock to be absorbed. Fluff up
with a fork.

2 Trim the courgettes at both ends
then cut into pieces about 2cm/1in
long. Slice into fine julienne strips with
a sharp knife. Halve the black olives,
discarding the stones (pits).

3 Carefully mix the courgettes, olives
and almonds into the couscous.

4 Blend together the olive oil, lemon
juice, coriander, parsley, cumin and
cayenne in a small bowl. Stir into the
salad, tossing gently to mix through.
Transfer to a large serving dish and
serve immediately.

THAI RICE SALAD

This is a lovely, soft, fluffy rice dish, perfumed with limes and fresh lemon grass. As well as being a good accompaniment for a family supper, it would be an excellent choice, in double or even triple the quantity, for a barbecue or buffet table.

SERVES FOUR

INGREDIENTS

2 limes
1 lemon grass stalk
225g/8oz/generous 1 cup brown long
  grain rice
15ml/1 tbsp olive oil
1 onion, chopped
2.5cm/1in piece fresh root ginger,
  peeled and finely chopped
7.5ml/1½ tsp coriander seeds
7.5ml/1½ tsp cumin seeds
750ml/1¼ pints/3 cups
  vegetable stock
60ml/4 tbsp chopped fresh
  coriander (cilantro)
spring onion (scallion) finely sliced,
  and toasted coconut strips,
  to garnish
lime wedges, to serve

1 Pare the limes using a zester or a fine grater, taking care to avoid cutting the bitter pith. Set aside the rind. Finely chop the lower portion of the lemon grass stalk and set aside.

2 Rinse the rice in plenty of cold water until the water runs clear. Tip it into a sieve and drain thoroughly.

COOK'S TIP
You could substitute the finely grated rind of kaffir limes for an authentic Thai flavour, but you will need to use juicier Tahitian or Mexican limes for cutting into wedges to serve.

3 Heat the olive oil in a pan. Add the onion, ginger, spices, lemon grass and lime rind and cook gently over a low heat, stirring occasionally, for about 3 minutes until the onion is soft.

4 Add the drained rice and cook. stirring constantly, for 1 minute, then pour in the stock and bring to the boil. Reduce the heat to very low and cover the pan with a tight-fitting lid. Cook gently for 30 minutes, then check the rice. If it is still crunchy, re-cover and leave for 3–5 minutes more. Remove the pan from the heat when done.

5 Stir in the fresh coriander, fluff up the grains, cover the pan again and leave for about 10 minutes. Transfer to a large serving dish or individual bowls, garnish with strips of spring onion and toasted coconut, and serve with plenty of lime wedges.

FENNEL, ORANGE AND ROCKET SALAD

THIS LIGHT AND REFRESHING SALAD IS IDEAL TO SERVE WITH SPICY OR RICH FOODS. ZESTY ORANGE BLENDS PERFECTLY WITH THE DELICATE FLAVOUR OF FENNEL AND THE PEPPERY ROCKET.

SERVES FOUR

INGREDIENTS
    2 oranges, such as Jaffa, Shamouti or
        blood oranges
    1 fennel bulb
    115g/4oz rocket (arugula) leaves
    50g/2oz/⅓ cup black olives
For the dressing
    30ml/2 tbsp extra virgin olive oil
    15ml/1 tbsp balsamic vinegar
    1 small garlic clove, crushed
    salt and ground black pepper

1 With a vegetable peeler, cut strips of rind from the oranges, leaving the pith behind, and cut into thin julienne strips. Cook in boiling water for a few minutes. Drain and set aside. Peel the oranges, removing all the white pith. Slice them into thin rounds and discard any seeds.

2 Trim the fennel bulb, then cut in half lengthways and slice across the bulb as thinly as possible, preferably in a food processor fitted with a slicing disc or using a mandolin.

3 Combine the slices of orange and fennel in a serving bowl and toss with the rocket leaves.

4 To make the dressing, mix together the oil, vinegar, garlic and seasoning. Pour over the salad, toss together well and leave to stand for a few minutes. Sprinkle with the black olives and julienne strips of orange. Serve.

VARIATION
Substitute minneolas for the oranges.

AUBERGINE, LEMON AND CAPER SALAD

LEMON SUBTLY UNDERLINES THE FLAVOUR OF MELTINGLY SOFT AUBERGINE IN THIS CLASSIC SICILIAN DISH. IT IS DELICIOUS SERVED AS AN ACCOMPANIMENT TO A PLATTER OF COLD MEATS, WITH PASTA OR SIMPLY ON ITS OWN WITH SOME GOOD CRUSTY BREAD.

SERVES FOUR

INGREDIENTS
    1 large aubergine (eggplant),
        weighing about 675g/1½lb
    60ml/4 tbsp olive oil
    grated rind and juice of 1 lemon
    30ml/2 tbsp capers, rinsed
    12 pitted green olives
    30ml/2 tbsp chopped fresh flat
        leaf parsley
    salt and ground black pepper

COOK'S TIP
This salad will taste even better when made the day before. It will keep well, covered in the refrigerator, for up to 4 days. Return the salad to room temperature before serving.

1 Cut the aubergine into 2.5cm/1in cubes. Heat the olive oil in a large, heavy frying pan. Add the aubergine cubes and cook over a medium heat for about 10 minutes, tossing frequently, until golden and softened. You may need to do this in two batches. Remove with a slotted spoon, drain on kitchen paper and sprinkle with a little salt.

2 Place the aubergine cubes in a large serving bowl, toss with the lemon rind and juice, capers, olives and chopped parsley and season well with salt and pepper. Serve at room temperature.

VARIATION
Add toasted pine nuts and shavings of Parmesan cheese for a main course dish.

VEGETABLE STIR-FRY IN LIME DRESSING

THERE IS NOTHING QUITE LIKE CRISP AND SWEET, YOUNG VEGETABLES. HERE, THEY ARE QUICKLY STIR-FRIED TO RETAIN THEIR TEXTURE AND THEN TOSSED IN A ZESTY LIME AND HONEY DRESSING.

SERVES FOUR

INGREDIENTS

15ml/1 tbsp groundnut
  (peanut) oil
1 garlic clove, sliced
2.5cm/1in piece fresh root ginger,
  peeled and finely chopped
115g/4oz baby carrots
115g/4oz patty pan squash
115g/4oz baby corn
115g/4oz green beans, trimmed
115g/4oz sugar-snap peas, trimmed
115g/4oz young asparagus, cut into
  7.5cm/3in pieces
8 spring onions (scallions), cut into
  5cm/2in pieces
115g/4oz cherry tomatoes
For the dressing
  juice of 2 limes
  15ml/1 tbsp clear honey
  15ml/1 tbsp soy sauce
  5ml/1 tsp sesame oil

1 Heat the groundnut oil in a large frying pan or wok. Add the garlic and chopped root ginger and stir-fry over a high heat for 1 minute, stirring the spices constantly.

2 Add the baby carrots, patty pan squash, baby corn and green beans and stir-fry for another 3–4 minutes.

3 Add the sugar-snap peas, asparagus, spring onions and cherry tomatoes, and stir-fry for a further 1–2 minutes. Use two wooden spoons or chopsticks to toss the ingredients, so that they cook evenly on all sides.

4 To make the dressing, add the lime juice, honey, soy sauce and sesame oil to a small bowl and stir to mix well. Add the dressing to the frying pan or wok and stir through.

COOK'S TIP
Stir-fries take only moments to cook so prepare this dish at the last minute to retain its crisp texture.

5 Cover the pan or wok and cook the vegetables for 2–3 minutes more, or until they are just tender but still crisp. Transfer to individual bowls or plates and serve immediately.

VARIATION
You can substitute other vegetables, such as baby leeks or fresh peas, but keep a balance of colour and flavour.

CALIFORNIAN CITRUS FRIED RICE

PINK GRAPEFRUIT ADDS ITS DISTINCTIVE FLAVOUR TO THIS DELICIOUS VEGETABLE, NUT AND CITRUS RECIPE. IT IS IMPORTANT TO MAKE SURE THAT THE COOKED RICE IS COLD BEFORE IT IS FRIED.

SERVES FOUR TO SIX

INGREDIENTS
  1 pink grapefruit or Jaffa orange
  4 eggs
  10ml/2 tsp Japanese rice vinegar
  30ml/2 tbsp light soy sauce
  about 45ml/3 tbsp groundnut
    (peanut) oil
  50g/2oz/½ cup cashew nuts
  2 garlic cloves, crushed
  6 spring onions (scallions),
    diagonally sliced
  2 small carrots, cut into
    julienne strips
  225g/8oz asparagus, each spear cut
    diagonally into 4 pieces
  175g/6oz/2¼ cups button (white)
    mushrooms, halved
  30ml/2 tbsp sake
  30ml/2 tbsp water
  450g/1lb/4 cups cooked white long
    grain rice
  about 10ml/2 tsp sesame oil
  thin strips of orange rind, to garnish
For the hot dressing
  5ml/1 tsp grated orange rind
  30ml/2 tbsp sake
  45ml/3 tbsp soy sauce
  30ml/2 tbsp freshly squeezed pink
    grapefruit or orange juice
  5ml/1 tsp medium or hot
    chilli sauce

2 Beat the eggs with the vinegar and 10ml/2 tsp of the soy sauce. Heat 15ml/1 tbsp of the oil in a wok and cook the eggs until lightly scrambled. Transfer to a plate and set aside.

3 Add the cashew nuts to the wok and stir-fry for 1–2 minutes. Set aside.

4 Heat the remaining oil and add the garlic and spring onions. Cook over a medium heat for 1–2 minutes, or until the onions begin to soften, then add the carrots and stir-fry for 4 minutes.

5 Add the asparagus and cook for 2–3 minutes, then add the mushrooms and stir-fry for 1 minute. Stir in the sake, the remaining soy sauce and the water. Simmer for a few minutes until the vegetables are just tender.

6 Mix together the ingredients for the dressing, then add to the wok and bring to the boil. Add the rice, scrambled eggs and cashew nuts. Toss over a low heat for about 4 minutes until the rice is warmed through. Just before serving, stir in the sesame oil and the grapefruit or orange segments. Garnish with strips of orange rind and serve immediately.

1 Cut a thin slice of peel and pith from each end of the grapefruit or orange. Place cut-side down on a plate and cut off the peel and pith in strips. Remove any remaining pith. Cut out each segment leaving the membrane behind.

VEGETABLE FAJITAS

LIME ADDS PIQUANCY AND ITS DISTINCTIVE FLAVOUR TO THE GUACAMOLE SERVED WITH THESE FAJITAS. FOR EXTRA TANG, WEDGES ARE SQUEEZED OVER THE TORTILLAS BEFORE EATING.

SERVES TWO

INGREDIENTS
  1 onion
  1 red (bell) pepper
  1 green (bell) pepper
  1 yellow (bell) pepper
  1 garlic clove, crushed
  225g/8oz/3¼ cups mushrooms
  90ml/6 tbsp vegetable oil
  30ml/2 tbsp medium chilli powder
  salt and ground black pepper
  coriander (cilantro) sprigs and
    1 lime, cut into wedges, to garnish
  4–6 flour tortillas, warmed, to serve
For the guacamole
  1 ripe avocado
  1 shallot, coarsely chopped
  1 fresh green chilli, seeded and
    coarsely chopped
  juice of 1 lime

1 Slice the onion. Cut the peppers in half, remove the seeds and cut the flesh into strips. Combine the onion and peppers in a bowl. Add the crushed garlic and mix lightly.

2 Remove the mushroom stalks. Save for making stock, or discard. Slice the caps and add to the pepper mixture.

3 Mix the oil and chilli powder in a cup, pour over the vegetable mixture and stir well. Set aside.

4 To make the guacamole, cut the avocado in half and remove the stone (pit) and the peel. Put the flesh into a food processor or blender with the shallot, green chilli and lime juice. Process for 1 minute, or until smooth. Transfer to a small bowl, cover closely with clear film (plastic wrap) and put in the refrigerator to chill until required.

5 Heat a frying pan or wok until very hot. Add the marinated vegetables and stir-fry over a high heat for 5–6 minutes, or until the mushrooms and peppers are just tender. Season to taste with salt and pepper.

6 Spoon a little of the filling on to each tortilla and roll up. Garnish with fresh coriander sprigs and lime wedges and serve immediately with the guacamole.

CHICKPEA TAGINE <u>WITH</u> PRESERVED LEMON

NUTTY-FLAVOURED CHICKPEAS ARE OFTEN USED IN MOROCCAN COOKING. HERE THEY ARE SLOWLY COOKED WITH TOMATOES AND SPICES, WITH PRESERVED LEMON ADDED JUST BEFORE SERVING.

SERVES FOUR TO SIX

INGREDIENTS

150g/5oz/¾ cup chickpeas, soaked
   overnight and drained, or 2 × 400g/
   14oz cans chickpeas, drained
30ml/2 tbsp sunflower oil
1 large onion, chopped
1 garlic clove, crushed
400g/14oz can chopped tomatoes
350ml/12fl oz/1½ cups
   vegetable stock
5ml/1 tsp ground cumin
¼ preserved lemon
30ml/2 tbsp chopped fresh
   coriander (cilantro)
salt and ground black pepper

1 If using dried chickpeas, simmer in plenty of water for 1–1½ hours until tender. Drain.

2 Skin the chickpeas by placing them in a bowl of cold water and rubbing them between your fingers.

3 Heat the oil in a pan and cook the onion and garlic for 8–10 minutes.

4 Add the chickpeas, tomatoes, stock and cumin and stir to mix well. Season well. Bring to the boil and simmer for 30–40 minutes, or until the chickpeas are completely soft and most of the liquid has evaporated.

5 Rinse the preserved lemon and cut away the flesh and pith. Use a sharp knife to cut the peel into slivers, then stir into the chickpeas along with the chopped coriander. Serve immediately with crusty bread.

DESSERTS

When people think about fruit desserts, citrus fruits do not immediately spring to mind, so the recipes featured here will probably come as a delightful surprise. There are, of course, traditional favourites such as chocolate mousse, while children never cease to enjoy the apparently magical surprise of a reversible sponge pudding swimming in a lovely, lemony syrup. However, there are lots of unexpected treats in store, from mandarin trifle and chocolate cones to familiar cheesecakes given a tangy citrus makeover.

LIME SABAYON WITH CHOCOLATE ICE CREAM

SABAYON SAUCE HAS A LIGHT, FOAMY TEXTURE THAT PERFECTLY COMPLEMENTS THE RICH, SMOOTH FLAVOUR OF ICE CREAM. THIS TANGY LIME VERSION IS DELICIOUS WITH CHOCOLATE ICE CREAM, BUT CAN ALSO BE SERVED WITH TROPICAL FRUIT, SOFT FRUIT OR VANILLA ICE CREAM.

SERVES FOUR

INGREDIENTS
  2 egg yolks
  65g/2½oz/5 tbsp caster
    (superfine) sugar
  finely grated rind and juice of
    2 limes
  60ml/4 tbsp white wine or
    apple juice
  45ml/3 tbsp single (light) cream
  500ml/17fl oz/2¼ cups chocolate
    ice cream
  thinly pared strips of lime rind,
    to decorate

1 Put the egg yolks and caster sugar in a heatproof bowl and beat well until thoroughly combined. Beat in the lime rind and juice, then the white wine or apple juice.

2 Whisk the mixture over a pan of simmering water until the sabayon is smooth and thick, and the mixture leaves a ribbon trail when the whisk is lifted from the bowl.

3 Lightly whisk in the cream. Remove the bowl from the pan and cover with a lid or plate.

4 Working quickly, place scoops of the chocolate ice cream into four chilled sundae glasses or individual serving dishes. Spoon the warm lime sabayon sauce over the ice cream, sprinkle with the strips of lime rind to decorate and serve immediately.

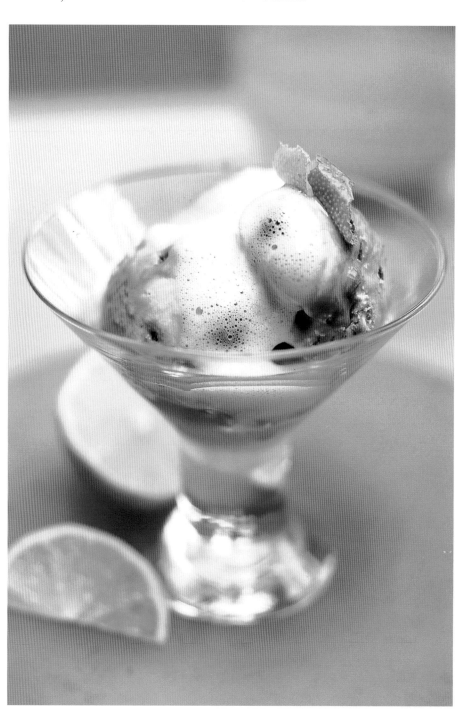

VARIATIONS
You can substitute other citrus fruit for the limes in the sabayon sauce. Orange sabayon, using the rind and juice of one orange, would also go well with chocolate ice cream, while lemon sabayon sauce complements peach sorbet (sherbet).

COOK'S TIP
For a special occasion, serve the ice cream in frosted glass. Rub the rim of the glasses with a lime wedge, then dip in a saucer of caster (superfine) sugar. Leave to dry before carefully adding the scoops of ice cream.

ICED LIME CHEESECAKE

THIS CHEESECAKE HAS A DELICIOUSLY TANGY, SWEET LIME FLAVOUR, BUT NEEDS NO GELATINE TO SET THE FILLING, UNLIKE MOST UNBAKED CHEESECAKES. IT IS NOT DIFFICULT TO PREPARE AND LOOKS PLEASANTLY SUMMERY WITH ITS FRESH CITRUS DECORATION.

SERVES TEN

INGREDIENTS
   175g/6oz almond biscuits (cookies)
   65g/2½oz/5 tbsp unsalted
      (sweet) butter
   8 limes
   115g/4oz/generous ½ cup caster
      (superfine) sugar
   90ml/6 tbsp water
   200g/7oz/scant 1 cup
      cottage cheese
   250g/9oz/generous 1 cup
      mascarpone cheese
   300ml/½ pint/1¼ cups double
      (heavy) cream

1 Lightly grease the base and sides of a 20cm/8in springform cake tin (pan) and line with baking parchment. Break up the almond biscuits slightly, then put them in a strong plastic bag and crush them completely with the side of a rolling pin.

2 Melt the butter in a small pan and stir in the biscuit crumbs until evenly combined. Spoon the mixture into the tin and pack it down with the back of a spoon. Freeze the biscuit mixture while you make the filling.

3 Finely grate the rind and squeeze the juice from five of the limes. Heat the sugar and water in a small, heavy pan, stirring constantly until the sugar has completely dissolved. Bring to the boil and boil for 2 minutes, without stirring, then remove the pan from the heat, stir in the lime juice and rind and leave the syrup to cool.

4 Press the cottage cheese through a sieve into a large bowl. Beat in the mascarpone, then the lime syrup. Lightly whip the cream and fold into the cheese mixture. Pour into a shallow container, cover and freeze until thick. If you are using an ice cream maker, add the cream and churn in the ice cream maker until thick.

5 Meanwhile, using a sharp knife, cut a thin slice of peel and pith from both ends of the each of the remaining limes. Place cut side down on a plate and cut off the peel and pith in strips. Remove any remaining pith. Cut the limes into thin slices.

6 Arrange the lime slices around the sides of the tin, against the parchment.

7 Carefully pour the cheese mixture over the biscuit base in the tin and level the surface with a round-bladed knife. Cover with clear film (plastic wrap) and freeze the cheesecake overnight.

8 About 1 hour before you are going to serve the cheesecake, carefully transfer it to a serving plate and put it in the refrigerator to soften slightly.

BASIL <u>AND</u> ORANGE GRANITA

*MORE OFTEN ASSOCIATED WITH SAVOURY DISHES, BASIL HAS A SWEET, AROMATIC FLAVOUR THAT
COMPLEMENTS TANGY ORANGES BEAUTIFULLY.*

SERVES SIX

INGREDIENTS
  5 large oranges
  175g/6oz/scant 1 cup caster
    (superfine) sugar
  450ml/¾ pint/scant 2 cups water
  orange juice (if necessary)
  15g/½oz/½ cup fresh basil leaves
  a few tiny fresh basil leaves,
    to decorate

1 Pare the rind thinly from three of the oranges and place the rind in a pan.

2 Add the caster sugar and water. Heat gently, stirring constantly until the sugar has completely dissolved. Remove from the heat and leave to cool, then pour into a bowl and chill.

3 Squeeze the juice from the oranges and pour it into a large measuring jug (cup). You should have about 600ml/ 17fl oz/scant 2¼ cups. If there is not enough, make it up to the required quantity with more fresh orange juice.

4 Pour the juice into a food processor or blender and add the basil leaves. Process the mixture until the basil has been chopped into very small pieces.

5 Using a slotted spoon, remove the orange rind from the chilled syrup. Stir in the orange juice and basil mixture, then pour into a large plastic tub or similar freezerproof container. Cover and freeze for about 2 hours, or until the mixture around the edges is just turning mushy.

6 Break up the ice crystals with a fork and stir well. Freeze for 30 minutes more until once again frozen around the edges. Break up with a fork and return to the freezer. Repeat the procedure until the ice forms fine crystals.

7 To serve, spoon the granita into chilled tall glasses and decorate with the tiny basil leaves.

COOK'S TIP
Ruby grapefruit could be used in place of the orange, if you wish.

STAR ANISE <u>AND</u> GRAPEFRUIT GRANITA

*WITH ITS ANISEED FLAVOUR, STAR ANISE MAKES AN INTERESTING ADDITION TO CITRUS FRUIT
DESSERTS, AND ITS DRAMATIC APPEARANCE MAKES IT THE IDEAL DECORATION. THIS REFRESHING AND
UNUSUAL GRANITA IS BOTH TANGY AND SWEET.*

SERVES SIX

INGREDIENTS
  200g/7oz/1 cup caster
    (superfine) sugar
  450ml/¾ pint/scant 2 cups water
  6 whole star anise
  4 grapefruit

1 Put the caster sugar and water in a small, heavy pan and heat gently, stirring occasionally, until the sugar has completely dissolved.

2 Stir in the star anise and heat the syrup gently, without stirring, for about 2 minutes, until slightly thickened and syrupy. Remove the pan from the heat and leave to cool.

3 Using a sharp knife, take a slice off the top and bottom of each grapefruit, then slice off the skin and all the pith. Chop the flesh coarsely and place it in a food processor. Process until almost smooth, then press the pulp through a sieve into a bowl.

4 Strain the syrup into the bowl of grapefruit purée, reserving the star anise. Mix well, then pour the mixture into a shallow freezerproof container. Cover and freeze for about 2 hours, or until the mixture starts to freeze and forms ice crystals around the edges of the container.

5 Using a fork, break up the ice crystals, then return the mixture to the freezer. Freeze for 30 minutes more, mash with a fork again, then return to the freezer. Repeat the process until the mixture forms fine ice crystals.

6 To serve, spoon the granita into glasses and decorate with the reserved star anise.

GRAPEFRUIT IN HONEY AND WHISKY

CREATE A SIMPLE YET ELEGANT DESSERT BY ARRANGING A COLOURFUL FAN OF PINK, RED AND WHITE GRAPEFRUIT SEGMENTS IN A SWEET WHISKY SAUCE. THIS DESSERT IS PERFECT AFTER A RICH MEAL.

SERVES FOUR

INGREDIENTS
  1 pink grapefruit
  1 red grapefruit
  1 white grapefruit
  50g/2oz/¼ cup sugar
  60ml/4 tbsp clear honey
  45ml/3 tbsp whisky
  mint leaves, to decorate

1 Cut a thin slice of peel and pith from each end of the grapefruit. Place cut side down on a plate and cut off the peel and pith in strips. Remove any remaining pith. Cut out each segment leaving the membrane behind. Put the segments into a shallow bowl.

2 Put the sugar and 150ml/¼ pint/ ⅔ cup water into a heavy pan, bring to the boil, stirring constantly, until the sugar has completely dissolved, then simmer, without stirring, for 10 minutes, until thickened and syrupy.

3 Heat the honey in a pan and boil until it becomes a slightly deeper colour or begins to caramelize. Remove the pan from the heat, add the whisky and, using a match or taper, carefully ignite, if you like, then pour the mixture into the sugar syrup.

VARIATION
The whisky can be replaced with brandy, Cointreau or Grand Marnier.

4 Bring to the boil, and pour over the grapefruit segments. Cover and leave until cold. To serve, put the grapefruit segments on to four serving plates, alternating the colours, pour over some of the syrup and decorate with mint.

ORANGES IN CARAMEL SAUCE

THE APPEAL OF THIS TASTY DESSERT IS THE CONTRAST BETWEEN THE SWEETNESS OF THE CARAMEL AND THE TANGY TARTNESS OF THE ORANGES. MAKE IT IN ADVANCE FOR CONVENIENT ENTERTAINING.

SERVES SIX

INGREDIENTS
 6 large seedless oranges, such
  as Navelina, well-scrubbed
 90g/3½oz/½ cup sugar

1 With a vegetable peeler, remove wide strips of rind from two of the oranges. Stack two or three strips at a time and cut into very thin julienne strips.

2 Using a sharp knife, cut a thin slice of peel and pith from both ends of each orange. Place cut-side down on a plate and cut off the peel and pith in strips. Remove any remaining pith. Slice the peeled fruit crossways into thick rounds about 1cm/½in thick. Put the orange slices in a serving bowl and pour over any juice.

3 Half-fill a large bowl with cold water and set aside. Place the sugar and 45ml/3 tbsp water in a small, heavy pan without a non-stick coating and bring to the boil over a high heat, swirling the pan to dissolve the sugar.

4 Continue to boil, without stirring, until the mixture turns a dark caramel colour. Remove the pan from the heat and, standing well back, dip the base of the pan into the cold water to stop the cooking process.

5 Add about 30ml/2 tbsp water to the caramel, pouring it down the sides of the pan, and swirl to combine.

6 Add the strips of orange rind and return the pan to the heat. Simmer gently over a medium-low heat, stirring occasionally, for 8–10 minutes, or until the strips are slightly translucent. Remove the pan from the heat.

7 Pour the caramel and rind over the oranges, turn gently to mix and chill for at least 1 hour before serving.

RICH CHOCOLATE MOUSSE WITH GLAZED KUMQUATS

THE COMBINATION OF CITRUS AND CHOCOLATE HAS ALWAYS BEEN A FAVOURITE. PERFUMED KUMQUATS, GLAZED IN AN ORANGE LIQUEUR SAUCE, MAKE THIS RICH CHOCOLATE MOUSSE EXTRA SPECIAL.

SERVES SIX

INGREDIENTS

   225g/8oz plain (semisweet)
     chocolate, broken into squares
   4 eggs, separated
   30ml/2 tbsp brandy or orange liqueur
   90ml/6 tbsp double (heavy) cream
For the glazed kumquats
   275g/10oz/2¾ cups kumquats
   115g/4oz/generous ½ cup
     granulated sugar
   15ml/1 tbsp orange liqueur, such as
     Grand Marnier

1 To make the glazed kumquats, halve the fruit lengthways and place cut side up in a shallow serving dish.

2 Place the sugar in a small pan with 150ml/¼ pint/⅔ cup water. Heat gently, stirring constantly, until the sugar has dissolved, then bring to the boil and boil rapidly, without stirring, until a golden-brown caramel forms.

VARIATION
Use peeled and sliced small, seedless oranges in place of the kumquats.

3 Remove the pan from the heat and very carefully stir in 60ml/4 tbsp boiling water. Stir in the orange liqueur, then pour the caramel sauce over the kumquat slices and leave to cool. Once completely cold, cover and chill.

4 Line a shallow 20cm/8in round cake tin (pan) with clear film (plastic wrap). Melt the chocolate in a bowl over a pan of barely simmering water, then remove the bowl from the heat.

5 Beat the egg yolks and brandy or liqueur into the chocolate, then gently fold in the cream. In a separate mixing bowl, whisk the egg whites until stiff, then gently fold them into the chocolate mixture. Pour the mixture into the prepared tin and level the surface. Chill for several hours until set.

6 To serve, turn the mousse out on to a plate and cut into slices or wedges. Serve the chocolate mousse on serving plates and spoon some of the glazed kumquats alongside.

CHOCOLATE MANDARIN TRIFLE

TRIFLE IS ALWAYS A TEMPTING TREAT, BUT WHEN A RICH CHOCOLATE AND MASCARPONE CUSTARD IS COMBINED WITH Amaretto di Saronno AND mandarin ORANGES, IT BECOMES SHEER DELIGHT.

SERVES SIX TO EIGHT

INGREDIENTS
  4 trifle sponges
  14 amaretti
  60ml/4 tbsp Amaretto di Saronno or
    sweet sherry
  8 mandarin oranges
For the custard
  200g/7oz plain (semisweet)
    chocolate, broken into squares
  30ml/2 tbsp cornflour (cornstarch)
  25g/1oz/2 tbsp icing
    (confectioners') sugar
  2 egg yolks
  200ml/7fl oz/scant 1 cup milk
  225g/8oz/1 cup mascarpone cheese
For the topping
  225g/8oz/1 cup ricotta cheese
  chocolate shapes
  mandarin orange slices

1 Break up the trifle sponges and place them in a large glass serving dish. Crumble the amaretti evenly over them and then sprinkle with the Amaretto or sweet sherry.

2 Squeeze the juice from two of the mandarins and sprinkle into the dish. Peel the remaining mandarins and remove and discard the pith. Cut out each segment leaving the membrane behind. Squeeze the remaining juice from the membrane and sprinkle into the dish. Add the segments to the dish.

3 Make the custard. Melt the chocolate in a heatproof bowl over a pan of barely simmering water.

4 In a separate bowl, mix the cornflour, sugar and egg yolks to a paste.

5 Heat the milk in a small pan until almost boiling, then pour on to the egg yolk mixture, stirring constantly. Return to the clean pan and stir over a low heat until the custard has thickened slightly and is smooth.

6 Stir in the mascarpone until melted. Add the melted chocolate, mixing it in evenly. Spread over the trifle sponges, cool, then chill.

7 To make the topping, evenly spread the ricotta cheese over the custard. Decorate with chocolate shapes and mandarin slices just before serving.

CHOCOLATE CONES WITH APRICOT SAUCE

THE SEDUCTIVE COMBINATION OF DARK CHOCOLATE WRAPPED AROUND A CREAMY BRANDY-FLAVOURED FILLING MAKES A DRAMATIC AND DELICIOUS DESSERT THAT IS SURPRISINGLY EASY TO MAKE. LEMON ADDS A SHARP EDGE TO THE SWEET APRICOT SAUCE THAT SURROUNDS THE CONES.

SERVES SIX

INGREDIENTS
250g/9oz dark (bittersweet)
  chocolate, broken into squares
350g/12oz/1½ cups ricotta cheese
45ml/3 tbsp double (heavy) or
  whipping cream
30ml/2 tbsp brandy
30ml/2 tbsp icing
  (confectioners') sugar
finely grated rind of 1 lemon
strips of thinly pared lemon rind,
  to decorate
For the sauce
185g/6½oz/⅔ cup apricot jam
45ml/3 tbsp lemon juice

1 Cut 12 double thickness circles, 10cm/4in in diameter, from baking parchment or paper and shape each into a cone. Secure with masking tape.

3 Stand each cone point downward in a cup or glass, to hold it straight. Leave in a cool place until the chocolate cones are completely set.

4 Make the sauce. Combine the apricot jam and lemon juice in a heavy pan. Melt over a low heat, stirring frequently, then remove the pan from the heat and set aside to cool.

5 Beat the ricotta cheese, cream, brandy and icing sugar in a small bowl. Stir in the lemon rind. Spoon or pipe the ricotta mixture into the cones, then carefully peel off the baking parchment.

6 Serve the chocolate cones in pairs on individual plates, decorated with lemon rind and surrounded with the cooled apricot sauce.

2 Melt the chocolate in a heatproof bowl over a pan of hot water, cool slightly, then spoon a little into each cone, swirling and brushing it to coat the paper in an even layer.

COOK'S TIPS
• When making the paper cones, make sure there is no gap at the pointed end, or the chocolate will run out when you coat them. It is best to let the chocolate cool slightly before use, so that it sets quickly.
• The cones can be made, filled and arranged with the sauce on plates before you start your meal, then chilled.

APPLE ᴬᴺᴰ KUMQUAT SPONGE PUDDINGS

*THE INTENSE FLAVOUR OF KUMQUATS MAKES THESE DAINTY PUDDINGS SPECIAL. SERVED WITH MORE
KUMQUATS IN A CREAMY SAUCE, THIS IS A DESSERT THAT IS SURE TO PLEASE.*

SERVES EIGHT

INGREDIENTS
    150g/5oz/10 tbsp butter, at room
      temperature, plus extra for greasing
    175g/6oz cooking apples, peeled and
      thinly sliced
    75g/3oz kumquats, thinly sliced
    150g/5oz/¾ cup golden caster
      (superfine) sugar
    2 eggs
    115g/4oz/1 cup self-raising
      (self-rising) flour
For the sauce
    75g/3oz kumquats, thinly sliced
    75g/3oz/6 tbsp caster
      (superfine) sugar
    250ml/8fl oz/1 cup water
    150ml/¼ pint/⅔ cup crème fraîche
    5ml/1 tsp cornflour (cornstarch)
      mixed with 10ml/2 tsp water
    lemon juice to taste

1 Prepare a steamer. Butter eight
150ml/¼ pint/⅔ cup dariole moulds or
ramekins and put a disc of buttered
baking parchment on the base of each.

2 Melt 25g/1oz/2 tbsp butter in a frying
pan. Add the apples, kumquats and
25g/1oz/2 tbsp sugar and cook over
medium heat for 5–8 minutes, or until
the apples start to soften and the sugar
begins to caramelize. Remove from the
heat and leave to cool.

3 Cream the remaining butter with the
remaining sugar until pale and fluffy.
Add the eggs, one at a time, beating
after each addition. Fold in the flour.

4 Evenly divide the apple and kumquat
mixture among the prepared moulds.
Top with the sponge mixture. Cover the
moulds and put into the steamer. Steam
for 45 minutes.

5 Meanwhile, make the sauce. Put the
kumquats, sugar and water in a pan
and bring to the boil, stirring to dissolve
the sugar. Simmer for 5 minutes.

6 Stir in the crème fraîche and bring
back to the boil, stirring. Remove the
pan from the heat and gradually whisk
in the cornflour mixture. Return the pan
to the heat and simmer very gently for
2 minutes, stirring constantly. Add
lemon juice to taste.

7 Turn out the puddings and serve hot,
with the sauce.

PASTRIES, CAKES AND BAKES

Small wonder that so many triumphs of the pastry chef's art are tarts and pies with tangy citrus fillings that contrast superbly with the rich, crisp crusts. Eggs, soft cheeses, cream, nuts and chocolate are just some of the ingredients that partner deliciously with lemons, oranges and limes. Dishes range from international classics and family favourites such as light jewelled fruit cake and Key lime pie to contemporary dishes such as a Sicilian ricotta cake.

KEY LIME PIE

THIS SPLENDID TART WITH ITS RICH LIME FILLING IS ONE OF AMERICA'S FAVOURITES. AS THE NAME SUGGESTS, IT ORIGINATED IN THE FLORIDA KEYS.

SERVES TEN

INGREDIENTS
  4 eggs, separated
  400g/14oz can condensed milk
  grated rind and juice of 3 limes
  a few drops of green food
    colouring (optional)
  30ml/2 tbsp caster (superfine) sugar
  thinly pared lime rind and fresh mint
    leaves, to decorate
For the pastry
  225g/8oz/2 cups plain
    (all-purpose) flour
  115g/4oz/½ cup chilled butter, diced
  30ml/2 tbsp caster (superfine) sugar
  2 egg yolks
  pinch of salt
  30ml/2 tbsp chilled water
For the topping
  300ml/½ pint/1¼ cups double
    (heavy) cream
  2–3 limes, thinly sliced

1 To make the pastry, sift the flour into a mixing bowl, add the butter and rub in with your fingertips until the mixture resembles fine breadcrumbs. Add the sugar, egg yolks, salt and water, then mix to a soft dough.

COOK'S TIP
You can make the pastry in a food processor, but you must take care not to overprocess the dough. Process the flour, butter and sugar first, then add the egg yolks and water. Use the pulse button and process for a few seconds at a time; switch off the motor the moment the dough gathers together.

2 Roll out the pastry on a lightly floured surface and use to line a deep 21cm/8½in fluted flan tin (tart pan), allowing the excess pastry to hang over the edge. Prick the pastry base with a fork and chill for at least 30 minutes.

3 Preheat the oven to 200°C/400°F/Gas 6. Trim off the excess pastry from around the edge of the pastry case (pie shell) using a sharp knife. If using a metal flan tin, you can just roll over the rim with a rolling pin. Line the pastry case with baking parchment or foil and baking beans.

4 Bake the pastry case blind for about 10 minutes. Remove the parchment or foil and beans and return the pastry case to the oven for 10 minutes more.

5 Meanwhile, beat the egg yolks in a large bowl until light and creamy, then beat in the condensed milk, with the lime rind and juice, until thoroughly combined. Add the food colouring, if using, and continue to beat until the mixture is thick.

6 In a grease-free bowl, whisk the egg whites to stiff peaks. Whisk in the caster sugar, then fold into the lime mixture.

7 Lower the oven temperature to 160°C/325°F/Gas 3. Pour the lime filling into the pastry case, smoothing the top. Bake for 20–25 minutes until it has set and is turning brown. Cool, then chill.

8 Whip the cream for the topping and spoon it around the edge of the pie. Cut each lime slice from the centre to the edge, then twist it and arrange between the spoonfuls of cream. Decorate with lime rind and mint leaves.

RICOTTA AND CITRUS CHEESECAKE TART

CHEESECAKE FILLINGS ARE EXCELLENT MADE WITH RICOTTA CHEESE BECAUSE RICOTTA HAS A GOOD, FIRM TEXTURE. HERE IT IS ENRICHED WITH EGGS AND CREAM AND ENLIVENED WITH TANGY ORANGE AND LEMON RIND TO MAKE A SICILIAN-STYLE DESSERT.

SERVES EIGHT

INGREDIENTS
   450g/1lb/2 cups low-fat ricotta
      cheese
   120ml/4fl oz/½ cup double
      (heavy) cream
   2 eggs
   1 egg yolk
   75g/3oz/6 tbsp caster
      (superfine) sugar
   finely grated rind of 1 orange
   finely grated rind of 1 lemon
   thinly pared and shredded orange
      and lemon rind, to decorate
For the pastry
   175g/6oz/1½ cups plain
      (all-purpose) flour
   45ml/3 tbsp caster
      (superfine) sugar
   pinch of salt
   115g/4oz/½ cup chilled butter, diced
   1 egg yolk

1 To make the pastry, sift the flour, sugar and salt on to a clean, cold work surface. Make a well in the centre and put the diced butter and egg yolk into it. Gradually work the flour into the diced butter and egg yolk, mixing with your fingertips until fully incorporated.

VARIATIONS
Add 50–115g/2–4oz/⅓–⅔ cup finely chopped candied peel to the filling in step 3, or 50g/2oz/⅓ cup plain (semisweet) chocolate chips. For a really rich dessert, you can add both candied peel and some grated plain chocolate.

2 Gather the dough together in your hand, reserve about a quarter for the lattice, then gently press the rest into a 23cm/9in fluted tart tin (pan) with a removable base. Chill the pastry case (pie shell) for 30 minutes and wrap and chill the reserved dough.

3 Meanwhile, preheat the oven to 190°C/375°F/Gas 5 and make the filling. Put the ricotta cheese, cream, eggs, egg yolk, sugar and orange and lemon rinds into a large bowl, and beat together until evenly mixed.

COOK'S TIPS
• The trick to making successful pastry, whatever the type, is to handle it as little and as lightly as possible.
• Use cold utensils. A marble rolling pin is ideal or buy one that can be filled with iced water.
• Don't skip the process of resting the reserved dough in the refrigerator. This will make it easier to roll out and to use as decorative lattice strips without it breaking apart.

4 Prick the base of the pastry case, then line with baking parchment or foil and fill with baking beans. Bake blind for 15 minutes, then transfer to a wire rack, remove the parchment or foil and beans and leave the tart shell to cool completely in the tin.

5 Spoon the cheese and cream filling evenly into the pastry case and level the surface. Roll out the reserved dough and cut into strips about 1cm/½in wide. Arrange the strips across the top of the filling in a lattice pattern, sticking them in place at the edges with a little water.

6 Bake for 30–35 minutes, or until golden and set. Transfer to a wire rack and leave to cool, then remove the side of the tin, leaving the cheesecake on the tin base. Carefully slide on to a serving platter and serve decorated with orange and lemon rind.

LIGHT JEWELLED FRUIT CAKE

FULL OF NUTS, CANDIED PEEL, FRESH CITRUS RIND AND DRIED FRUITS, THIS MOIST CAKE MAKES IDEAL CHRISTMAS FARE. DECORATE IT WITH A PRETTY RIBBON, IF YOU LIKE.

SERVES SIX TO EIGHT

INGREDIENTS

115g/4oz/½ cup currants
115g/4oz/⅔ cup sultanas
  (golden raisins)
225g/8oz/1 cup quartered glacé
  (candied) cherries
50g/2oz/⅓ cup finely chopped mixed
  candied peel
30ml/2 tbsp rum, brandy or sherry
225g/8oz/1 cup butter
225g/8oz/generous 1 cup caster
  (superfine) sugar
finely grated rind of 1 orange
finely grated rind of 1 lemon
4 eggs
50g/2oz/½ cup chopped almonds
50g/2oz/½ cup ground almonds
225g/8oz/2 cups plain
  (all-purpose) flour
50g/2oz/⅓ cup whole
  blanched almonds
30ml/2 tbsp apricot jam, warmed

1 Soak the currants, sultanas, glacé cherries and the mixed peel in the rum, brandy or sherry in a large bowl. Cover with clear film (plastic wrap) and leave for a few hours but ideally overnight.

2 Grease and line a 20cm/8in round or an 18cm/7in square cake tin with a double thickness of baking parchment.

COOK'S TIP
This cake can be stored for up to two weeks. Do not remove the paper before cooling as it helps to keep the cake moist. Store in an airtight container.

3 Preheat the oven to 160°C/325°F/ Gas 3. In a large bowl, whisk the butter, sugar and orange and lemon rinds together until they are light and fluffy. Beat in the eggs, one at a time.

4 Add the chopped almonds, ground almonds, soaked fruits (with their liquid) and the flour, and mix to make a soft dropping (pourable) consistency. Spoon into the tin. Bake for 30 minutes.

5 Gently arrange the whole almonds in a pattern on top of the cake. Do not press them into the cake or they will sink during cooking. Return the cake to the oven and cook for a further 1½–2 hours, or until the centre is firm to the touch. Let the cake cool in the tin for 30 minutes, then remove it and let it cool completely on a wire rack. Remove the paper and brush the top with a little warmed apricot jam.

PANETTONE

THIS ITALIAN BREAD IS A WELL-LOVED CHRISTMAS TREAT. IT IS SURPRISINGLY LIGHT EVEN THOUGH THE DOUGH IS RICH WITH BUTTER, CANDIED PEEL AND DRIED FRUIT.

SERVES SIX TO EIGHT

INGREDIENTS
150g/5oz/10 tbsp butter, softened,
   plus extra for greasing
400g/14oz/3½ cups unbleached
   strong white bread flour, plus extra
   for kneading and dusting
2.5ml/½ tsp salt
15g/½oz fresh yeast
120ml/4fl oz/½ cup lukewarm milk
2 eggs
2 egg yolks
75g/3oz/6 tbsp caster
   (superfine) sugar
oil, for greasing
115g/4oz/⅔ cup mixed chopped
   candied citrus peel
75g/3oz/generous ½ cup raisins
melted butter, for brushing

1 Using a double layer of baking parchment, line and butter a 15cm/6in deep cake tin (pan) or soufflé dish. Extend the paper 7.5cm/3in above the top of the tin or dish.

2 Sift the flour and salt together into a large bowl. Make a well in the centre. Cream the yeast with 60ml/4 tbsp of the milk, then mix in the remainder.

3 Pour the yeast mixture into the well in the centre of the flour, add the whole eggs and mix in sufficient flour to make a thick batter. Sprinkle a little of the remaining flour over the top and leave in a warm place for about 30 minutes to "sponge" – when the yeast begins to bubble through the flour covering.

4 Add the egg yolks and sugar and mix to a soft dough. Work in the butter, then turn out on to a lightly floured surface and knead for about 5 minutes, or until smooth and elastic. Place in a lightly oiled bowl, cover with oiled clear film (plastic wrap) and leave to rise, in a warm place, for 1½–2 hours, or until doubled in bulk.

5 Knock back (punch down) the dough and turn out on to a lightly floured surface. Gently knead in the candied peel and raisins. Shape into a ball and place in the prepared tin or dish. Cover with lightly oiled clear film and leave to rise in a slightly warm place for 1 hour, or until doubled in size.

COOK'S TIP
Once the dough has been enriched with butter, do not leave to rise in too warm a place or the loaf will become greasy.

6 Meanwhile, preheat the oven to 190°C/375°F/Gas 5. Brush the surface of the dough with melted butter and cut a cross in the top using a sharp knife. Bake for 20 minutes, then reduce the oven temperature to 180°C/350°F/Gas 4. Brush the top with butter again and bake for a further 25–30 minutes, or until golden. Cool in the tin or dish for 5–10 minutes, then turn out on to a wire rack to cool.

SICILIAN RICOTTA CAKE

ORANGE LIQUEUR AND GLACÉ CITRUS PEEL MAKE THIS TRADITIONAL CAKE OF LAYERED RICOTTA CHEESE TRULY IRRESISTIBLE AND THE PERFECT CHOICE FOR A DINNER PARTY DESSERT. START PREPARATIONS THE DAY BEFORE, AS THE CAKE NEEDS TO BE CHILLED.

SERVES EIGHT TO TEN

INGREDIENTS
675g/1½lb/3 cups ricotta cheese
finely grated rind of 1 orange
150g/5oz/¾ cup vanilla sugar
75ml/5 tbsp Cointreau or other
  orange liqueur
115g/4oz/½ cup glacé (candied)
  citrus peel
8 trifle sponge cakes
60ml/4 tbsp freshly squeezed
  orange juice
extra glacé (candied) citrus peel,
  to decorate

1 Push the ricotta cheese through a sieve into a bowl with a wooden spoon, add the orange rind, vanilla sugar and 15ml/1 tbsp of the liqueur and beat well to mix. Transfer about one-third of the mixture to another bowl, cover and chill until ready to serve.

2 Finely chop the citrus peel and beat into the remaining ricotta cheese mixture until evenly mixed. Set aside.

3 Line the base of a 1.2 litre/2 pint/ 5 cup loaf tin (pan) with baking parchment. Cut the trifle sponge cakes in half horizontally. Arrange four pieces of sponge side by side in the base of the loaf tin and sprinkle with 15ml/ 1 tbsp each of liqueur and orange juice.

4 Spread one-third of the ricotta and fruit mixture evenly over the sponge layer. Cover with four more pieces of sponge and sprinkle with another 15ml/ 1 tbsp each of orange liqueur and orange juice as before.

COOK'S TIP
Baking parchment, sometimes called non-stick baking paper, has largely replaced greaseproof (waxed) paper for lining cake and loaf tins (pans). It is made from paper and contains heat-resistant silicon, giving it an extremely effective non-stick surface. Although more expensive than greaseproof paper, it is more efficient and is especially useful with mixtures containing a high proportion of sugar.

5 Repeat with the alternate layers of ricotta mixture and sponge until all the ingredients are used, soaking the sponge pieces with liqueur and orange juice each time, and ending with a soaked-sponge layer. Cover the cake with a piece of baking parchment.

6 Cut a piece of thin cardboard to fit inside the tin, place on top of the baking parchment and weigh down evenly. (Use a couple of cans of fruit or tomatoes.) Chill for 24 hours.

7 To serve, remove the weights, cardboard and baking parchment and run a palette knife (metal spatula) between the sides of the cake and the tin. Place a large serving plate on top of the tin, then invert the two, holding them firmly together, so that the cake is upside down on the plate. Peel off the lining parchment.

8 Spread the chilled ricotta mixture over the cake to cover it completely, then decorate the top with citrus peel, cut into fancy shapes. Serve chilled.

VARIATIONS
• Use mandarin or tangerine juice instead of orange and replace the orange liqueur with Mandarine Napoléon.
• Add 25g/1oz/¼ cup finely chopped pistachio nuts and 30ml/2 tbsp chopped glacé (candied) cherries to the ricotta mixture in step 2.
• Add 30ml/2 tbsp chopped stem (preserved) ginger in step 2.

CLEMENTINE SHORTBREAD FINGERS

LIGHT AND MOUTHWATERING, THESE CITRUS SHORTBREADS ARE A REAL TEA-TIME TREAT. MADE WITH CLEMENTINES THEY MAKE SUBTLY SWEET FESTIVE FARE.

MAKES EIGHTEEN

INGREDIENTS
   115g/4oz/½ cup unsalted (sweet)
      butter, plus extra for greasing
   50g/2oz/¼ cup caster (superfine)
      sugar, plus extra for sprinkling
   finely grated rind of 4 clementines
   175g/6oz/1½ cups plain
      (all-purpose) flour, plus extra
      for dusting

VARIATION
Substitute the grated rind of one Ugli fruit for the clementine rind and sprinkle the shortbread fingers well with sugar before baking.

1 Preheat the oven to 190°C/375°F/ Gas 5 and grease a large baking sheet with butter. Beat together the butter and sugar until soft and creamy, then beat in the clementine rind.

COOK'S TIP
The shortbread fingers will keep in an airtight container for up to 2 weeks.

2 Gradually add the flour and gently pull the dough together to form a soft ball. Roll out the dough on a lightly floured surface to about 1cm/½in thick.

3 Cut into fingers, sprinkle over a little extra sugar and put on to the baking sheet. Prick with a fork and bake for 20 minutes, or until light golden brown.

CINNAMON AND ORANGE TUILES

THESE DELIGHTFUL FRENCH BISCUITS ARE GENTLY AROMATIC WITH THE ADDITION OF CINNAMON AND ORANGE. DIP THEM IN GOOD QUALITY CHOCOLATE FOR AN ELEGANT FINISHING TOUCH.

MAKES FIFTEEN

INGREDIENTS
  2 egg whites
  90g/3½oz/½ cup caster
    (superfine) sugar
  7.5ml/1½ tsp ground cinnamon
  finely grated rind of 1 orange
  50g/2oz/½ cup plain
    (all-purpose) flour
  75g/3oz/6 tbsp butter, melted
For the dipping chocolate
  75g/3oz Belgian plain
    (semisweet) chocolate
  45ml/3 tbsp milk
  75–90ml/5–6 tbsp double (heavy)
    or whipping cream

1 Preheat the oven to 200°C/400°F/ Gas 6. Line three large baking trays with baking parchment.

2 Whisk the egg whites to soft peaks, then whisk in the sugar until smooth and glossy. Add the cinnamon and orange rind, sift over the flour and fold in with the melted butter. Add 15ml/ 1 tbsp freshly boiled water.

3 Place 5 spoonfuls of the mixture on each tray. Flatten and bake, one tray at a time, for about 7 minutes, or until golden. Cool briefly, then remove with a spatula and roll around the handle of a wooden spoon. Cool on a rack.

4 To make the dipping chocolate, place the chocolate in a small pan and pour in the milk. Heat very gently, stirring constantly, until the chocolate has melted and the mixture is smooth, then stir in the cream.

5 Dip one or both ends of the biscuits (cookies) in the chocolate and leave to cool on wire racks.

COOK'S TIP
If you have not made these before, cook only one or two at a time until you get the hang of it. If they harden too quickly to allow you time to roll them, return the baking sheet to the oven for a few seconds, then try rolling them again.

INDEX

Bibliography

The Oxford Companion to Food
by Alan Davidson,
Oxford University Press,
Oxford, 1999

Jane Grigson's Fruit Book by
Jane Grigson, Penguin Books,
London, 1982

Citrus Varieties of the World by
James Saunt, Sinclair
International, revised and
updated, Norwich, 2000

Picture Acknowledgements

The publishers would like to
thank the following companies
for the loan of their pictures:

The Art Archive p6tr, p9bl

The Bridgeman Art Library
Still life of grapes, oranges
and a peeled lemon by
Gillemans, Jan Pauwel the
Elder (1618–75), Johnny
van Haeften Gallery,
London, UK p6bl

Garden Picture Library
p20, 21, 23, 29

Garden Wildlife Matters
p14, 22tr

Mary Evans Picture Library
p7tr and b, p9tr

V & A Picture Library p8.